# A Basket of Goodies

## Ingredients for a Better World

# F.G. Ghamsari

Quantum Discovery
A LITERARY AGENCY

A Basket of Goodies
Copyright © 2023 by F.G. Ghamsari

ISBN
978-1-961601-01-7 (Paperback)
978-1-961601-02-4 (eBook)

*To my wife, Monica; my daughter, Jasmine, and all the members of my family and to all people who sacrifice their lives to help others without monetary expectation or recognition—people who are working hard for freedom and economy, empowering the needy around the world without engagement to benefit or to benefit a government or beneficiaries of the world's gigantic global economic machine.*

*To the Iranian America Jewish community outside Iran whose exertion to preserve the Iranian language, tradition, culture, and heritage in recent decades is visible and indefatigable.*

# TABLE OF CONTENTS

A Basketful of Goodies

Subjects in this Book Would Propound a Question, Who Is
Right and Who Is Wrong in Our Divergent Worlds?

Observations of an Iranian American in this World's Arena.

F. G. Ghamsari

# INTRODUCTION

We have come a long way from the times when prosperous Western countries colonized and divided the rest of the world among themselves, robbing from other nations their natural resources and wealth. We have come a long way from the Dark Ages, even from a relatively recent time of slavery, when "laborers" were not compensated for their hard work, and basic human rights were ignored or denied. We have come a long way from the times when people traveled by way of horses, camels, donkeys, or elephants and from times where there were no lights, radios, telephones, or televisions; no roads or cars; and none of today's unprecedented advancements in technology, machinery, and medicine.

The world owes a great deal of gratitude to visionaries, such as master Mahatma Gandhi, for his heroic, peaceful demonstrations that infused the inception of changes around the world, and Dr. Martin Luther King, who followed in Gandhi's footsteps to bring freedoms to black citizens of the United States of America and help them transcend their former plights of injustice. The world is also indebted to innovators and scientists whose diverse inventions facilitated improved living conditions worldwide.

We have come a long way, but in reality, the more changes are made, the more conditions have remained the same and, in some cases, mutated and worsened. We have left the colonization era behind, but now we see smaller countries getting slapped in the face, often without reason, by stronger nations who have developed sophisticated bombers, as well as unprecedented combat weapons. The era of slavery has past, but now a new type of slavery has been born—a slavery in which people worldwide must maintain two jobs in order to keep up with expenses and their local runaway economies and taxes. Even entire countries are facing economic predicaments due to out-of-reach deficits and the money supply by a constant borrowing, which is going around and around for now, until one day that due to unablity to borrow could not go around any more.

We no longer use animals for travel, and each day thousands of amazing airplanes can be seen flying over the continents and the oceans, arriving at their destinations in a matter of hours. Hundreds of millions of automobiles and other vehicles transport products or people from one point to another, using a vast array of roads. This mass of movement requires energy, and the source of energy usually contains various petroleum products. Due to excessive use of these petroleum products, an abundance of carbon monoxide is thrown in the air, menacing the atmosphere and endangering human life, as well as the future of mother earth. Marketing and capitalization of these products are becoming a source of amplifying revenue for many countries as well as many oil companies and has become a pillar to the world's economy. Many governments or regimes are replaced and people are killed by one or more superpower countries to faciliate the flow of these products. Sadly, as the globe's scientific communities have pointed out over and over, much illness and suffering and even death are contributed to the use of these products. Even though the new EV technology can be a gate to freedom from fossil fuel however as is today cannot offer a lasting alternative. First problem is that lifetime of each charging is too short preventing across the country or a long distance driving. Secondly, if there is a mass charging it would create a black out as the electricity manufacturers are not ready to compensate the technology. Another obstacle is the required elements in making batteries and their locations of obtainment.

Life has many inconveniences, some made by governments, some made by religions, some made by public habitants and some made by individuals. A host of problems and augmentations gathered in this book as well as recommendations that may offer solutions. Gun control, religion domination, rich and poor and I especially recommend reading two parts, The Economic Machine and The Minimum Wage Increase.

The citizens of certain nations enjoy the establishment of the highest achievement of civilizations—human rights, freedom, and democracy. However, some nations provide only a degree of this triumvirate, while other nations do not provide them at all. The degree of freedom in nations varies from a very high level in one nation to nonexistent in another. Nevertheless, these wonderful words, *freedom* and *democracy*, have become tools in the hands of some Western nations to achieve their goals, and when their goals are achieved, the condition of human rights no longer matter. The terms *political influences, interferences, intrusions, occupations, aggressions,* and *domination* do not define freedom in any language. And yet, these things have occurred in the name of freedom, human rights, and democracy over and over throughout the world.

Governing a country is a difficult task, and some governments do so fairly, while others are brutal. Any government, however, will go to any length to protect itself from falling. Let's assume that there is an uprising against a government in one of the so-called modern or first world countries. My guess is that those behind the insurgency would get the same treatment as those in so-called third world countries. In other words, the definition of government today contains not only "to govern" but also "to dictate orders to a nation at anytime, anywhere usually at all costs and in a first or third world countries the treatments would be the same."

In this dog-eat-dog world, nevertheless, the integral goal of religious concepts is justice for all. This same justice that was manifested in the Ten Commandments of Moses, in the teachings of Zoroaster, in the teaching of Jesus, in the teaching of Mohammed and all other prophets that have profoundly influenced the notions. Despite all these religious teachings, philosophical ideas, and the passage of thousands years, the simple ideals of love and justice for all do not prevail among humankind or among nations. A leader of one nation calls that of another government "the Great Satan." The rival government refers to the first (along with a group of nearby nations) as the "axis of evil." We do not see much love shared between the leaders of these two nations. No common denominator has been established among different groups of people with diverse ideologies, religions, nationalities, races, and beliefs. As said by the eminent freedom advocate, the exalted Gandhi, "I have an inconsumable passion for truth and love." Whatever love may have once existed is today vanishing, due to classifications among religions and belief systems, racism, unrepresented interaction and migration, misunderstandings, financial responsibilities and complexities, cultural clashes, and the greed of individuals, governments and corporations.

The United States gave me an opportunity and a place to live, and I am forever grateful for that. Though I do assert that I live in the best country the world offers, my expectation of what the "best" means has often, unfortunately, not measured up to my experiences—I have witnessed too many instances in which one would expect more from the best. Each administration would have it own domestic and foreign policies, some beneficiary to humanity and some which would result in disasterous conditions.

Religion plays a big role in our lives and in societies. The belief system that informs one's childhood is so strong for many that, for the rest of our lives, we lack courage to question our beliefs. Thus, most of us are never able to deny our convictions in our lifetimes. A section of this book belongs to this forbidden subject.

It is appalling to see that the world does not know much about the contributions made by Iran to advance our world into today's modern world. It would be important for me to offer a limited knowledge in regards to these contributions. My hope is that this brief can at least present some understanding of Iran's role throughout history and draw a picture to clarify some of misunderstandings about Iran.

Through time and life, we collect experiences. Experiences fetch us knowledge. Thus, time and life are the most effective sources of knowledge. For the most part, the information here depends on personal experiences, which may or may not be the exact reality. However, I did not purposely manipulate any issue to make a right wrong and a wrong right, and whatever I am saying I believe to be the truth and real.

The style I used is not strictly expository, descriptive, persuasive, or narrative, but perhaps it is a combination of all with a tendency toward narrative. However, as the great Frank Sinatra said, "I did it my way."

Now and then or whenever a subject interested me, I tried to write for my daughter all my knowledge about the subject, with a desire to leave something behind for her. I did not have any intention to write a book when I began writing for her. After she grew up, she became more and more busy, leaving her with a little time for my writings. Nevertheless, I thought my hours and hours of thinking and writing might become useful to others. I decided to compile them, and thus was born *A Basketful of Goodies*.

*Farhang G. Ghamsari*

# Views And Experiences

# 1

# A Worldwide Disarmament

There are some people who strongly believe that members of internationally formed organizations govern our world and that its order is secretly decided behind the curtain. To support such an idea, we can refer to the Council on Foreign Relations, England's Royal Institute of International Affairs, Bilderbergers, the Trilateral Commission, and so forth, each having its members with its own financial activities and agendas. Though the possibility of secrecy and conspiracy remains, here we look at the world as if the world is governed the way it appears to be.

Our world needs many social, political, and economical changes to benefit a greater percentage of the population than those who prosper today. We need a global disarmament plan to rid the planet of guns, biological weapons, bombers, missiles, and military personnel. The money and technology wasted on armaments should be diverted to projects that will save hungry children, shelter the homeless, and eliminate poverty. The funds should be invested in the development of devices to clear pollution, facilitate the growth of crops in deserts, create rain and snow, manufacture cheaper medicines, and purify drinking water. With them, we should devise plans to control the unsustainable global population growth and cure cancer. We must also create environmentally friendly vehicles and plans to reduce the massive vehicle usage that is one of the most significant contributors to global warming.

In short, we must facilitate life now and secure everyone's future so that people will not have to kill themselves working in order to provide for themselves and their families. We must provide a healthy global future, rather than spending so much money on defense budgets and on "war toys", such as the Intruder, the Eagle, the Black Hawk, the Nighthawk, the Stealth Bomber, the B-1, the F-1 bomber, and hundreds of other jets and bombers made all around the world, each costing humanity millions of dollars. This war game does not stop by the weapons of destruction but we can add the perilous cyber attacks into it as well, which can disable or kill us in a manner of minutes. We must plan to establish and maintain peace at every corner of the earth.

Today is May 7, 2023; the news is surrounding yet another mass shooting in Texas, where innocent people were killed. Most of the time, talks on both sides of the aisle are to protect the Second Amendment rather than protecting the innocent lives. According to the statistics, there are more firearms in the United States than there are people. Even though a great percentage of citizens do not own a gun, others own more than one. There are more people killed in the United States by guns than killed in all wars that this nation had involved in combined. The United States accounts for 5% of world population yet people own 45% of worldwide guns. There are two thousand gun shows per a year and during the COVID - 19 more guns purchased than at any times in the US history when 691 mass shooting occurred. It is also important to refer to a report by Los Angeles Times, June 19 2015. "This is a nation in which, in 2012, there were 1.2 million violent crimes," According to ATF gun manufacturing in the United States averages 11 million per a year. One cannot wonder who will purchase these firearm and for what besides killing.

With regard to the Second Amendment of the United States Constitution, it is obvious that our forefathers drafted the amendment during a time when US citizens were living differently than we are today. Houses were built apart from each other with big ranches in between, perhaps like the good old Bonanza television show, or people lived in the woods. City life was limited to a handful of houses in each city, and citizens often fell prey in the hands of merciless gunmen who robbed the working class. These conditions are depicted in hundreds of once popular cowboy movies that show the citizens' fear upon the arrival of one of those characters in their cities.

In such an environment, the Second Amendment was born of the necessity of enabling citizens to defend themselves. Today, city life has grown. Millions of houses are built next to each other in hundreds of cities, and life's conditions have changed as well. Cowboy movies in which a character saves a whole city, which were popular twenty or thirty years ago, aren't even made anymore. So why do we continue to need to guns? Times have changed, and conditions are different. The law should follow suit.

If the monstrous defense budgets set by almost all governments around the world are computed to a dollar amount, it would be enough to eliminate world hunger and poverty and transcend most human suffering. However, most governments have agendas other than dealing with human suffering, and all of them are deeply involved with their own plans—plans that often have wrong results, wasting the nation's wealth and sometimes causing loss of lives. Most likely, the global economy is set up in such a way that a great portion of the worldwide wealth must revolve around armaments, which is a shame.

Sadly, some families from South America, Central America, or other parts of the world sell their young children into prostitution to help raise funds to buy their way into the United States. What is wrong with our world today? What is wrong with the wealth distribution and the economic movement of this world? And what is wrong with the unprecedented armament budgets and the encircled arms race facing our world today?

It is worth mentioning that the Communist system of government, despite all of its advancements in armament buildups, was nothing but a failure.

Our world needs a big brother to take our hands and show us how to walk toward a peaceful world, where people never have to leave their towns, cities, states, or countries in order to provide for themselves and their families. We need a new leader, who will show us how to use our lands and resources to feed ourselves without thinking about self-interests, one who does not terrorize us with sophisticated, manufactured weapons, bombing our cities by day and night, when we need to calmly sleep. Our world needs a leader who thinks about us, rather self-interests. We need kindness rather than violence, friendship rather than animosity, and love rather than hate. We need a big brother who is no one but us, humanity. It is rather childish to wait for a spiritual person called by different names among various religions to come down from the sky or emerge from a hidden place to fix our world. The big brother we need might be an internationally elected body in which all or none have the veto power. Such a body would be fair to all and not influenced by a few powerful nations; it would walk us toward an everlasting peace, which God has promised us in the holy books.

These kinds of ideas are seemingly out of order in our world today. This may not be true even a hundred years from now. However, religiously or logically, it is presumed that humanity is one body. If a part of one's body is aching, the pain will disable other parts of the body as well. Today, humanity's body is unbalanced and sick, perhaps mutated since a thousand years ago. It seems that new advancements and new technologies are unable to cure this sickness. In fact, new technologies have opened a bigger gap between the rich and the poor—a gap that has widened so much that some people grow fatter every day by overeating, while starvation leaves others with nothing but skin and bones. This is sick and unjust.

There is no question that the rich and the poor have always existed. Today, this separation is more visible than ever before. One reason is that the people who did not have still do not have. Some are busy with their goats and sheep, while others are without anything at all, living in primitive conditions. On the other hand, the rich have more than ever. "By looking at the media, social media and the spread of online access we can see" that the remote control style of life is available to people with money. The residents of Beverly Hills, California, seem to care less about what is happening to the residents of, for example, Haiti or Somalia. They would not agree to swap residencies with people living in other parts of the world. To have a mansion with twenty-eight bedrooms, indoor and outdoor swimming pools, and so forth is a dream. Less than 1 percent of the world's population will fulfill such a dream, while the other 99 percent die dreaming about it.

Nevertheless, a dream does not convey a reality, and it is only a dream. Thus, I do not have any conviction or belief in dreams. I believe in realities, and I believe that the wealth of nations ought to be somehow divided among all its citizens, rather than being primarily owned by a handful of opportunistic or lucky individuals. Of course, the rich always claim they worked very hard for their money. In reality, by working hard, no one gets rich, a fact to which people in different occupations around the globe can readily attest.

With the exception of a limited United Nations peacekeeping force, all military and civilian weapons should be destroyed. This request may be unreasonable, unreachable, or undesirable now. However, I can foresee that one day our world have no other choice than to put down all its weapons. Then, and only then, will great peace be possible. I do not claim to have the power to see the future, but common sense tells me about the future of arms and a disarmament that will have to come in the future. In my mind and with a great conviction, I have no doubt about the future of arms.

# 2

# A Zeal For Peace Or War

In addition to the loss of life, which no one can replace and no one can put a price on, war brings many tragedies. Among these are as babies losing their fathers, fathers and mothers losing their children, sisters losing their brothers, wives losing their husbands, and civilians or soldiers losing their arms, legs, and other body parts. The list goes on and on. War also brings distraction of different kinds. It interferes with one's way of life and with culture, art, wealth of civilians as well as the country, and much more. In a matter of seconds, people lose their houses, workplaces, and the things they have worked their lives to accumulate. They lose their daily food, cooking habits, and family gatherings. They lose their environment, conveniences, customs, and so forth.

It is said that war brings prosperity. Despite the prosperity that a war may bring, I do not like to see a war unless there are immediate dangers to people's lives, such as the cleansing policies in Kosovo, Germany, and Turkey, when other nations must rescue innocent people at all costs. Aside from these conditions, there is no reason or justification for war. Still, there are rulers who cannot wait for war; others do not have war on their agendas.

I think war is humanity at its lowest point, when a strong nation practices its strength on a weaker nation in order to fulfill its demands and interests. This practice is nothing new. It can be traced to the Persians, the Romans, and the Greeks and even to the Babylonian era almost 2,500 years ago and even before that. This aggressive, savage act has become much more dangerous in our new civilization, as with progress had come the development of technology and, with it, armaments. Today, there exist sophisticated weapons that could wipe out the planet earth in a matter of a few hours. The problem that I see here is that in 2,500 years of civilization, humanity did not make any advancement toward disarmament, but the same barbaric concepts still exists, with the most dangerous toys in the hands of the big boys.

Though politicians give 101 reasons to justify going to a war, to me, one life lost in a war is too many. I do not understand how members of an administration can appear on television with their proud faces when they have just caused innocent children, mothers, fathers, and friendly soldiers to lose their lives. To me, this is a shame, not a victory. What does a dead soldier need a citizenship certificate for, when he or she is dead? He is dead. In neither heaven nor hell will anyone ask for the certificate. How can we send nineteen-year-old men and women into a war to get killed? It is unnecessary, and whatever amount of money we give to their families will not be enough.

On the other hand, it takes billions of dollars to bring a war zone back to the same conditions as it was in before a war, and the public has to pay for it. Sometimes there are things lost in a war that can never be replaced. In addition, it is for the people of a nation to replace their government; it is not for another nation to step in for the purpose of replacing a government.

I remember after the revolution in Iran, The looters took away the leftover wealth of the country, and some dealers who took advantage of the situation are perhaps living very comfortably. I read somewhere that there was an exhibit of the Anions art held in Tokyo, Japan, few years ago; two large rooms filled with ageless Iranian (Persian) antiques. I was not there to see how much the art dealers had paid for these pieces but we can assume that many good deals were at hands. Here again we can see how some counties stay economically strong while others have no chance in this world.

I think that war is another method of wealth manipulation. Strong nations build up armament in certain nations and then destroy them in order to earn more revenue. Examples are all over the club, and for anyone who follows the news knows what I am talking about.

We talk about "Operation Freedom," but if we leave the people of the country we invaded alone and provide them with 100 percent freedom to elect their government, in my opinion, they will elect the most radical anti-Western leader. This is their freedom. This is another reason I believe war is a complete waste.

In conclusion, I believe that, for world peace, some regimes need to be removed, but I agree with the antiwar demonstrators—"War is not the answer."

It is also important to point out that we should not confuse two different issues that usually become confusing when a war begins. To support the troops is one thing, and to be antiwar is another thing. One thing has nothing to do with the other. I think that one who is antiwar supports the troops more than people who are for a war, because he or she does not want them to be killed.

# 3

# Diesel Fuel

There are many arguments among the pros and cons of dangering the environment, the ozone and the preservation of the greenhouse layer. It is obvious that healthy air and a healthy environment would guarantee life now as well as in the future. Many books describe unhealthy smoke, smog, and the dangerous chemicals thrown in the air by various means every day, creating a menace to the atmosphere. In California, the law is one step ahead of that in many other parts of the world by requiring a smog check set by the Department of Motor Vehicles. Though one can ask many questions about the applications of the law, and whether it is working or is not would be a different subject, at least there is an established law that has to be followed.

It is notable to see some politicians who are ecology minded making passionate statements and those others who do not concern themselves with this issue. Nevertheless, violation of the rules of Mother Nature are visible throughout cities every day, with thousands of polluting factories, as well as aircraft, and automobiles. Global warming is a challenge that humans face today, and environmentalists foresee a sad future if air pollution problems continue to exist.

Though these conditions are very severe in the United States, in other parts of the world, air pollution is much worse. In many large cities, especially capitals, the air is so full of carbon monoxide and exhaust fumes that breathing is difficult and can result in serious illnesses, if not immediate death. The problem is that, in the majority of these larger cities, mass transportation operates on diesel fuel. By mass transportation, I mean school buses, city buses, vans, construction equipment, fire department trucks, post office trucks, and on and on. All of these vehicles legally spew garbage into the air every day. Some politicians believe diesel fumes are not dangerous to our health. Others say that diesel fumes aren't as bad as gasoline fume. Many questions surround determining the difference between one smoke and another. Even if one is exposed to the most natural smoke, which is from burning wood for a long time, that person could get sick. How much worse the smoke of various chemicals could be is unimaginable.

Whatever view politicians may have, I think the high profit margin generated from diesel fuel has contributed massively to our global warming problem.

Despite any positive view toward diesel fuel, its smoke is very unhealthy and dangerous. I worked around LAX for a while, and I know that exposure to diesel fumes, even over a short period of time, results in headaches. I cannot even imagine the results of long-term exposure. I invite those who want to challenge me about the danger of diesel fumes to hold their heads next to the exhaust pipe of a smoky vehicle consuming diesel fuel (or even one that is not smoky) for a few minutes several days.

Why are we allowing our cities to be filled with diesel fuel smoke? Why are we exempting these poisonous vehicles from a control? Why are they exempt from the smog check in California?

Environmentalists are making valid arguments about the global warming, then why don't they look into the diesel fume problem in the United States and all around the world?

# 4

# Merchant And His Parrot

In the old days, there was a merchant who had a parrot. The parrot, in addition to being very beautiful, was very smart, and the merchant's customers grew to like it. The merchant sometimes had things to do, and he would leave the parrot in charge of the store until he could return. Of course, in those days, unlike today, there were not many robberies, especially in small villages such as the one where this story took place. The parrot knew that, when the owner was not there, no one could take any merchandise from the store and would say to the customers, "Hello. The owner will be back very soon. Please wait."

Many people who were familiar with the operation would either wait or go home and came back later. Others who did not know anything about the operation would either go away or wait for the merchant.

One day, when the merchant had to leave, a cat chasing a mouse entered the store. The parrot, who had never seen an attacking cat, grew scared and began to fly all over the store. As it was flying, its feathers accidentally hit a large jar of almond oil, knocking it off its perch. The big jar broke, leaving oil and broken glass on the floor where it had fallen. The sound of breaking scared the cat, and it quickly ran away.

When the owner came back, he did not at first notice anything different, and he went and sat down on his seat. Then he looked around and saw the broken jar and the spilled oil on the ground. He looked at the parrot and realized that its feathers were covered with oil. He told himself that the parrot must have broken the jar. He became angry, and taking a stick, he hit the parrot over the head and threw it in the corner of the store.

The parrot's head was bleeding, and a piece of its skin came off. After an hour or so, the merchant became very sad and sorry for what he had done. He attended the parrot with medicine and started to talk, but the parrot, which believed itself innocent, kept quiet and did not say a word.

Every day, the merchant cleaned the parrot's wound and put medicine on its head. But after the parrot's skin grew back, it became bald. Still, it would not talk. No matter what the merchant or the customers would say, the parrot would not say a word. The parrot had been the merchant's best friend—every day, it had talked to him and helped him with his business—and he deeply regretted his action. But the parrot still said nothing.

Many customers asked the merchant why the parrot was so quiet, and he would say that the parrot had broken the jar, spilled the oil, gotten hit with the stick, gone bald, and lost its speech. He said this story so many times that the parrot learned it word by word. It said, "Broke the jar, spilled the oil, got hit, and went bald." When the parrot had a chance, it would go by the mirror, look at its bald head, and say, "Broke the jar, spilled the oil, got hit, and went bald."

One day, a few friends gathered near the store and were talking among themselves. It happened that one of them was also bald. When the bald man went away, others said, "We know him, and up to a few years ago, he had lots of hair. We do not know what had happened to him or why he went bald."

At this time, the parrot suddenly opened its mouth. "Broke the jar, spilled the oil, got hit, and went bald," it said.

The people around became joyful that the parrot had finally spoken. And they laughed to think that it was thinking so much about its own baldness that it had, by comparison, concluded that all bald creatures had encountered the same occurrence.

The merchant was full of joy, and that day was one of his happiest days. His parrot was talking again.

Extracted and translated from Rumi's *Mathnawi-i Ma'nawi*

# 5

# My Bank Visits

It is a Monday morning in February 1970. I am entering the Security Pacific Bank at the corner of Western Avenue and Santa Monica Boulevard in Los Angeles. Though I am an unimportant customer of the bank, John the assistant manager knows me and calls me by my first name. Despite the fact that I am only a student and without a good job, he speaks with Mr. Wilson the branch manager to see if they can give me my first credit card. Everyone working at this bank is very nice, cooperative, and polite. The executives are mostly males, though there are female tellers behind the counter as well. There is a branch of Bank of America across the street, where the operation is more or less the same as that of Security Pacific Bank. My stay at the bank is short and pleasant, and it leaves me with a good feeling that I take home. After this visit, every now and then, when I need to go to the branch, the bank employees treat me like I am somebody special, which I am not.

Now, it is a Monday morning in February 2007. I am entering the Home Savings of America at the corner of Vermont and Hollywood Boulevard in Los Angeles. I have some questions or requests, and in order to be seen by someone, I have to write my name down on a waiting list. I am lucky to find a seat to sit in after writing my name down. Fifteen minutes passes, and there are still some people ahead of me, each as unhappy as I am. I ask the security personnel if I can see the manager. He replies that she is busy in a meeting, and he takes me to another female executive who gives me the runaround. I go back and sit down, waiting for my name to be called.

Years later in March 2023, I needed to visit my bank. It was there that I witnessed the same mistreatments floor personnel seemed to own the bank. It was at that time that I recalled my past experiences and realized the difference between then and now. I am unaware of the reason for these changes. Thereupon, it is important to point out that, in these last three or four decades, life has become extremely different. All the extra services are eliminated, and rudeness has replaced them, along with higher prices. For example, then, when you wanted to buy gasoline at the gas stations, an attendant checked you tire pressure and oil level, washed your windshield, and pumped your gasoline. Today, you have to go inside to pay politely, go back out to the gas pumps and pump your own gasoline, and leave politely. Price increases between then and now are visible in just about every product.

Thirty years ago, people did not have to kill themselves working in order to survive. Especially in the United States, despite a constant claim by the government that inflation is in control, we see every day that the prices are going up. For example, in 1970, a gallon of gasoline cost about twenty-seven cents, and the gas stations would even give you five times blue or green redeemable stamps. The individual greed, the greed of corporate America, the growth plans of executives and large-scale investors, accounting inputs, and deregulation policy have all changed, eliminating many of the good things of the past here in the United States, as well around the globe. Stress and depression are on the rise; we have higher crime rates, higher addiction rates, and higher homeless rates; and many other psychosocial problems seem to have replaced the calmness of the past.

The question is, are these complex social problems worth fighting to solve? I do not know, but I know that, in the past, life was extremely nice and much easier than it is now.

# 6

# My Dear Daughter

---

My dear daughter, as the time goes on, I wish to leave you something of my learned experiences. You can refer to it once in a while, or as you wish, or whenever you want to remember me. here are some specific points I'd like to share with you.

Note that the most important influences in early life beside parents and teachers, are friends, and such an influence is often greater than any other source. This friendship influences are so powerful that it can make or break you. It is said in the old times that a bad friend is worse than an enemy because you already know what to expect from an enemy. But from a friend you do not expect any unpleasant experiences, and that is why maintaining a relationship with a bad friend is so dangerous. It is said that a smart friend makes you smart, and a fool makes you a fool. So be very selective when it comes to who will be your friend.

In my opinion, there are three kinds of friends—those who always have time for you, those who never have time for you and want you to spend your time on them, and those who sometimes have time for you and sometimes do not. In other words, there are friends who want you for you, friends who want you for them, and friends who are in between. You will find that it would be best to have smart friends and friends who always have time for you.

It is so important to point out to you that the most precious jewel in life is life itself and nothing else. There is no other phenomenon as valuable as life—nothing that can be considered next to it or compared with it. Neither all the gold nor all the money in the whole world can match it; even love is worthless if there is no life. With all respect to those who gave their lives to change the world, do not give your life for anything because often nothing will change. It is understandable that we give our lives away to earn a living; there is no way to get around or beside that. Cherish and enjoy your life because it only happens once. You can buy gold, jewelry and even the world's most important elements—the air, the light, the soil, and the water, the four essentials of nature—but you can never buy time, which is the essence of life. Stay healthy and spend your worldly resources to eat well and to stay strong physically and emotionally at all times.

Life is very short. By the time we become aware that life is so precious, the old age will arrive unexpectedly. It will be too late to change anything we have done with our lives then. Follow a path that will not induce regrets at the old age. Take advantage of moments that will bring happiness, success, and satisfaction in the future. Do this for yourself and also do things that will positively affect others' lives. Life is very short. Setting aside what the various religions have told us, who is to say if, in reality, there is a heaven and a hell after life? Though I want to be a religious person and accept blindly all that religions tell us, this logical mind of mine is always arguing with me. Therefore, I think we have to be good for the good of the universe rather than expecting a place in heaven, and if there is a heaven in the end, we will attend it. If everybody, from diverse socioeconomic levels and political arenas, were good and honest we would have a better world than the one we have. Ideologies coming from different sources are good but often create division, animosity, and separation. So be good for the goodness of the world.

Do not postpone today's work for tomorrow. Accomplish today's work today and do tomorrow's work tomorrow.

Do not borrow money from anyone except from banks. Borrowing money from people will harm your character, moral standards, ethics, and grace. Do not lend money to anyone either, as it often becomes impossible to get it back.

If someone wishes to argue with you, turn your face another way and separate yourself from that person. An argument often results in a fight.

Spend according to your income and do not spend more than your earnings, as doing so will result in financial difficulties.

Regardless of how much money you have, it would be all right once in awhile to live as though you are poor. Then you will know how poor people live, and you will be helpful to them and appreciative of what you have.

Do not speak argumentatively, sarcastically, and with bad intention; if you do, you will not find many friends. Speak softly, with kindness, and sweetly; this will protect you.

Avoid aggressions and becoming involved with problems. You do not need the stress, and getting involved will create difficulties that may sometimes prove difficult to overcome.

Do not worry. Worrying does not solve a potential discomfort. Think and find a way to overcome a predicament.

Smile, as smile has lots of friends. On the other hand, anger has no friends.

Live the best possible way and enjoy your life to the fullest, because this journey is only one way.

Do not make a judgment before you see something with your own eyes. Other eyes can be misleading or dishonest.

Make a conclusion based upon logic and reasoning rather than emotions.

Be kind and friendly to everyone all the time. At the same time, defend your rights at all the times. Do not let anyone demand anything of you, attempt to take your rights away, or try to take advantage of your friendly attitude. What belongs to you belongs to you only. Stay away from abusive and demanding people as soon as you become aware of their behaviors.

My dear daughter, share your passions with others and every time you have something to say, write it down:

Write and write. Maybe your writings will eliminate discrimination.

Write and write. Maybe your writings will make the weak strong and the poor wealthy.

Write and write. Maybe your writings will make happy the heart of a lonely child.

Maybe you will make the world a better place.

Maybe you will feed the hungry and cure an ill.

Maybe your missives will fall into the heart of an abusive leader and occupy it fully with love and fidelity.

Maybe they will bring a smile to the face of a person who desperately needs a smile.

Maybe they will make way for the discovery of a cure for a disease that kills.

Maybe your words will prevent tears from being shed.

Maybe they will resolve economic problems around the world.

Maybe they will cure social pains.

Maybe they will free an addict from addiction.

Maybe what you say will cause nations to overcome disputes.

Maybe your writing will assist a needy person.

Maybe it will overcome moral and ethical corruptions.

Maybe it will retain and maintain a healthy living environment.

Write and write. Maybe your writings will limit the gap between rich and poor.

Write and write. Maybe your writings will dissolve the differences between followers of different religions.

Write and write. Maybe your writings will eliminate division between humankind.

This brief is a token of fatherly love. I hope that you will learn from it one or two matters that will assist you to have a wonderful life and that you might pass it on to your children if you chose to. I love you very much and thank you for accompanying me in life.

# 7

# My First Car

I was getting tired of missing the bus and hitchhiking, so I decided to save enough money to buy a car. It was a beautiful spring day in 1971, and I was going to work from school. When I got off the bus, there was my car sitting on White Oak Avenue with a "For Sale" sign on it. Something in my heart told me that it was going to be mine. It was a 1957 Chevy Bel Air convertible, and the asking price was $186. In those days, that was a fair market value, and I had enough money to buy it. The car needed a paint job and a new convertible top, but I did not mind the way it looked so long as it would take me to the places I needed to go. I called the owner, and bought the car in that same afternoon. No more hitchhiking, no more buses, and no more depending on other people.

Gasoline was very cheap in those days. Regular gas was about twenty-six cents per gallon, and premium cost twenty-nine cents per gallon. At gas war times, it was even a few cents cheaper. Gas stations would give away blue or green trading stamps according to the gallons of gasoline one would buy. People took their accumulated stamps to designated shops and redeemed them for appliances, blankets, and household products. The more stamps one had, the more merchandise he or she could receive for free.

Later on, gas companies wanted to increase their profits. They raised the price of gasoline, little by little to the current prices. It was all about profitableness and an excuse to justify price increases.

When the price of gasoline went up, it seems like the price of everything else went up as well. Before long the streets were filled with more homeless people, more gang members, and more crime and social discomfort than ever before.

Before the gasoline price soared people were relaxed, and we didn't have the stress and social or psychological problems of today. Everything was nice. Life was easy, and the language of music was love.

I sold my car for $200 after a year and half. I thought at the time that I'd made a good deal. Today, the identical car in mint condition is worth around $40,000 or more, which makes me wish I'd never sold it and I am missing the good old times.

Comparably, life has become extremely expensive, and many social predicaments are the result of these unsettling circumstances or unjust conditions for the poor. Unprecedented inventions, innovations, new technologies, and new products are in the marketplace, available for purchase by those who have the money to do so. At the same time, the levels of psychosocial problems and social diseases have rapidly increased, and more people than ever before complain about depression, stress, anxiety, and other psychosocial dilemmas.

In the eyes of many people, we are much better off today than we were before. In the eyes of many others, all of these advancements are not worth a minute of those good old days when one could sit all day under a tree and listen to the relaxing sounds of nature if he or she chose to do so. I do not know the answer, and even if I did, it is too late to turn around and go back. Maybe some politician, some billionaire, some do-gooder, a businessman or an ordinary person can find the way to combine the best of both worlds in the future.

# 8

# My Hitchhiking Days

It is about 11:00 p.m. on a Friday in 1970. I am at the corner of Ventura Boulevard and Tampa trying to go home. I do not have a car yet and have to rely on public transportation, mainly the buses or hitchhiking. I like to take the bus because it gives me a chance to read and do some of my homework on the way to or from home, which takes about an hour either way. I live in Hollywood, and going back home is more difficult because, late at night, the buses do not run as frequently. Hitchhiking is very popular, especially among the hippies, who find it their preferred way of getting around, and getting rides is easy.

I just got off work, and the bus left a few minutes before I finished. It will be about an hour, and sometimes it takes even longer, before the next bus will arrive. I prefer to hitchhike, rather than waiting. Most of the time, the people who pick me up are hippies with their own philosophies about politics and life. My opinion of them is that, if they can help you they will, and the action of helping others humbles me. I am still waiting for someone to come and give me a ride.

Before long, a late model car arrives, and gentleman wearing a suit and tie offers me a ride. I open the door and get in the car. After greeting him, I say, "Thank you so much for giving me a ride, sir."

The gentleman begins to drive, and we have some short and occasional conversations, mostly questions and answers, and almost pass the intersection of Tampa and Ventura Boulevard. He tells me that, with my education and good looks, I should not be working in a gas station. Then he says he has lots of connections and friends who are working in different oil companies, and he could help me get a better job—an offer that could change my life overnight. Then he begins to attempt conversing in a sexual manners, and little by little now, he is reaching out with his right hand.

We are approaching Barham Boulevard, which is not too far from Hollywood where I live. I am moving my body to the farthest side of the front seat and almost gluing myself to the passenger door. It quickly came to my mind that I had to go to my sister's house because her husband was working, and she was alone. He dropped me off at the corner of Hollywood Boulevard and Highland and gave me a piece of paper with his telephone number on it, saying that I could call him anytime I wanted to. I thanked him a lot, and as soon as I was dropped off, I ran home like I'd never run before.

After this incident, I tried to avoid hitchhiking, especially because it seemed to becoming increasingly dangerous. Awful stories of terrible things happening to hitchhikers in different parts of the country became all-too-familiar.

Today's lifestyle is a far cry from those good old days of my youth, so much so that comparison brings nothing but sadness.

# 9

# One-Way Street

I remember one fall evening in the late 1980s. After a day spent in Tijuana, I was returning to San Diego, accompanied by an old friend, Mickey. There is a street in Tijuana called Revolución, which eventually leads a traveler to the border. We were traveling north on Revolución, when suddenly, Mickey noticed a restaurant offering shrimp cocktails for a reasonable price. He asked me to turn around so he could buy some of those shrimps before we were out of Tijuana. He insisted so much that I did not pay attention to a one-way street sign and entered a street heading in the wrong direction. It was a short while, about fifty yards, before I realized I was driving on the wrong side of the street, but it was too late to turn around, as the flashing lights of a policeman were behind me. I knew that, if you got caught for any supposed violation in Mexico, you could buy your way out. I began negotiating with the officer, and Mickey finished the deal with a payment of thirty dollars. We forgot all about the shrimp cocktail and found our way out quickly. When we were in the States, we were thankful and happy that we had gotten away so easily.

One day, in Long Beach, California, where street traffic signs are also confusing, I was pulled over. The officer told me about my rights and said that, by signing the ticket, I was not admitting any guilt. He and I both knew he was only doing his job, and I had no problem with it. If I'd had a problem, which I didn't, there wasn't much I could have done about it. I signed the ticket, accepting my alleged guilt and left. One can go to traffic court to fight the ticket where, in majority of times, one is found guilty anyway, making it a waste of time. However, here in the United States, a so-called modern country, that is how the law works. the traffic law often offers you something, completely aware that all the odds are against you.

There was no sense in my going to the traffic court, where I had no chance of beating the ticket, so I mailed in the fine.

One day, I was passing through the streets of Beverly Hills and saw that part of a major street was blocked and police officers were directing traffic to go around using an altered route. My instant curiosity wanted to know why people were being directed away from the block. I later discovered that the street had been shut down to accommodate the birthday party, ceremony or, celebration of some wealthy person, perhaps a movie star.

On another day, I was passing through another street in Los Angeles and saw that a person was having a private party, and valet parking personnel had been paid to post "No Parking" signs all over the *public* street. I was surprised to see that money can buy a lot, but you have to have lots of it.

I immediately thought of my incident in Mexico and reflected that, in a smaller country, there is a chance for a poor person to buy the police as well, but here, only the rich and powerful people are able to have their wishes compensated.

It is necessary to mention that, I am not trying to advise anyone to break the law anywhere but the purpose is only a comparison.

If you have money here in the United States, the police will block the entire street for you. If you don't, you'll have to go around the block so that the rich man can have his party!

# 10

# One Heart Two Places

There is a common struggle among people who have left their birthplace to pursue a better life in another country. This struggle involves getting used to a new set of custom and losing the culture to which the newcomer is accustomed. It is about customs, and it is about cultures. This struggle is ongoing and constant, so much that some people cannot deal with it, and despite losses of money and dreams, they go back to their birthplace, where they feel comfortable with the customs. Those who stay abroad try to associate with their own people or to transfer their customs into their new home. Some try to make it on their own. In any case, the souls of many belong to their race, heritage, and nationality even though they emigrate abroad. By embracing freedom and new economic opportunities outside their birthplace, which were their two main reasons for leaving, they become two different souls in one body. The words of the old song from Neil Diamond, "between two shores, LA is fine but is not home," perfectly describe many people living in foreign lands' state of mind.

A person in this condition loves the old traditions, customs, culture, history, and literature of his or her former life and, at the same time, loves the freedom the new country has to offer. I am referring to freedoms offered in many Western countries, such as freedom of speech and religion. Nothing else is free anywhere, anyway.

# 11

# Story Of A Donkey

In the old days, a man traveled from village to village riding his donkey. During the days, he would look at the beautiful countryside, enjoying himself by sightseeing, and at nights, he would find a temple to sleep in. He was unmarried, alone, and poor. He had no skills, but he was a good speaker. He made his life based on traveling from one village to the next, speaking, reading poems, and talking about high moral standards. In return, he would receive some money from his audiences. He was happy with his life and thanked the Lord for the opportunity given to him. The donkey was his best friend and perfect company, taking him here and there to see the good and the bad that the world had to offer. He would say, "People are not going to stay hungry. God will somehow provide for His children, and no worries are necessary."

One day, he was passing through a desert and became hungry, thirsty, and tired. Then fortunately, he saw a village from afar, and he rushed into it. He drank from the first stream of clean water he found, and he had his donkey drink as well. He looked around the village, ate some food, and then began to look for a temple where he could sleep. When he found a temple, he realized there was some kind of celebration going on inside. He took his donkey to a man in charge of the stable and went to the party.

After the party was over with and many people had gone, those people who remained continued with the celebration and singing of songs. Most were homeless and, having nowhere to go, intended to stay overnight in the temple. They found out that the man who had joined them owned a donkey and planned to steal it from him. In order to steal the donkey, they made up a song, "Happiness arrived. Misery is gone. Happiness arrived. Misery is gone. The donkey is gone. The donkey is gone."

The man started to like the song, but he had no idea what the song was about. Soon he was singing the same song, and his singing became so fervent that he started to dance with the song. After all the singing and dancing, he became very tired and fell asleep.

The thieves took the donkey from the stable and sold it.

In the morning, the man wanted to leave and went to the stable to claim his donkey.

In response to his query, the donkey keeper told him that the donkey was gone.

"What do you mean?" the man demanded angrily.

"Your friends came and told me to come and see what you were singing and dancing," the donkey keeper explained. "And you were singing, 'The donkey is gone. The donkey is gone.' I thought that was what you wanted done."

The man realized what a mistake he had made, but it was too late. He realized that he should not follow others blindly or imitate people without knowing what their intentions might be.

Extracted and translated from an old Iranian story.

# 12

# The Robbers

During the years I've lived in the United States, along with being burglarized and a victim of auto theft, I was also robbed by gunpoint twice. The first time was in the early 1970s, when I was a student and working part-time as a parking attendant in a small parking lot in downtown Los Angeles. Around 10:00 a.m., the lot was usually full, and it remained relatively quiet until late afternoon. There was a booth behind the entrance that contained some equipment and a safe to drop the big bills in, along with any money exceeding the change the company provided. In addition, the booth contained a sign that read "Lot Full," which was to be placed at the entrance when the lot was full.

One day, around 10:30 a.m., when the lot was completely full, a man drove in by going around the sign in a copper Cadillac. I approached him and tried to let him know that the lot was full. He looked at me and said, "Give me all you got."

My English was not all that good in those days, and I could not understand what he was saying, especially given his pronunciation and how rapidly he was speaking.

He repeated, "Give me all you got."

And I repeated, "the lot is full."

The exchange of these words went on between us several times.

Finally, he was tired of it and said, "I got something hot."

I did not understand and thought that he wanted to sell or give me some hot food to eat and told him, "No thank you. I am not hungry."

The man showed me the top of the gun he was referring to and said, "Are you stupid? Give the money man."

I had never seen a gun in my life before. Then I realized what was happening. My legs started to shake. I handed him the company's change bag, as that was the company's policy for dealing with a robbery.

The man was asking me for the big bag, which I did not have.

Fortunately, at this time, another car was entering the lot, and the robber, apparently not wanting to be seen, squealed out of the lot. That was the last day I worked in the lot, as the fear the episode had induced in me would not leave me alone for a few days.

The second time I was robbed at gunpoint happened on my way home from school. I drove into the parking garage of the building where I used to live. My classes were at night, and the last class was done by 10:00 p.m. So I was usually home by 10:30, sometimes 11:00 if I stayed around talking with my classmates. That night, after I parked my car and started making my way to my apartment, I saw two strange, young males who seemed to be looking around for something or someone.

I said hello and tried to pass them quickly but one of them jumped into my path and started to ask me questions. He asked if I knew some females, who perhaps went by the names Linda or Jennifer. He asked if I knew where they lived. As I was responding to their question, assuring them that I did not know anyone with those names who lived in this apartment complex, suddenly the other male pointed a gun toward me. He reached out and ripped off the gold chain I was wearing around my neck.

The other man began searching in my pockets for valuables. He took out my wallet and took the forty or fifty dollars cash I had in it. Soon after, seeming to have gotten what they were looking for, they ran off toward the street.

Quickly, I went back to my car and began following them. Fortunately, there was a policeman sitting in his car across the street, and I was very happy to see him. I hoped that he would be able to help me right away. I approached him and explained what had happened to me, noting that the guys who'd robbed me were running away across the street. I thought he would follow them right away and recover my belongings, but I did not know how the law and the police department work.

The police officer asked me to get in his backseat, which I did, hoping he would go after the thieves. Instead, the officer took out a form and started to fill it out with all kinds of information, of which I was the provider. What color clothes were my attackers wearing? What was the color of their shoes? Were they wearing hats? The questions went on and on.

Then he radioed the incident in to his office and asked for backup. I realized that, by the time he finished with these formalities, the thieves were going to be home free. At that time, I told him I was tired and did not feel good and wanted to go home, if it was okay by him. He asked for my address and telephone number to let me know if my belongings were recovered and then let me go.

I realized my mistake. I should not wear jewelry anywhere on the streets of Los Angeles. I told myself that it could had been a lot worse, and I thanked God as victims usually do.

I never heard anything from the police or anybody else regarding my belongings or the thieves.

# 13

# The Shuttle Driver

There was this man who used to work for the company I was working for. He drove the company's shuttle bus, and for some unknown reason he quit his job and left the company. I did not see him for some time, maybe one or two years. One day, I went to a gas station on the way home and was surprised to see him pumping gasoline into a nice, late-model car. I was happy to see him, especially when I saw that he had a completely new look and a new image. After the usual exchange of greetings, I let him know that I was happy to see him, in particular with his new look. I figured he was driving somebody around and, out of curiosity, asked him who the car belonged to. He did not seem to like my question and told me that the car was his. He'd had his own business for a while, and the business had been good to him. I did not want to ask him what kind of business he had gotten into, and with a gesture, I showed him my gladness for him. He gave me one of his business cards and told me to call him to go for a lunch one of these days, stepped into his beautiful car, and left.

Seeing people's lives changes for the better in this dog-eat-dog world is interesting and uplifting, and I found myself thinking about the driver for a while after our chance meeting. Then one day, I saw a mutual friend who told me all about the man who I'd seen driving an expensive car instead of his old Toyota. He told me that our old friend's cousin worked in a city around Los Angeles as a supervisor or manager of the transportation and parking division, and he was the one who'd helped him win a transportation line contract.

Winning a city contract is a life-changing experience, and having a cousin who works in city hall is always helpful. Perhaps this kind of deal goes on at all governmental levels all around the world. And perhaps the higher the position one has, the bigger the bite available to one's family members or people close to him or her. I do not know and I have not been there to experience such a life-changing experience.

The way I was given the information about the shuttle driver was that the city wanted to provide a shuttle service to take elderly and handicapped persons to their doctors appointments' and to provide for their other transportation needs. My friend received the contract to provide such a service, for five or six years. He bought five vans and spent so much per year to pay rent, employees' salaries, insurance, gasoline, and communication equipment expenses. Of course, it is not of my concern and affair to know about the income and revenue of the business, but I think that's not a bad day at work.

City life—it is full with lots of know-how to take advantage of the opportunities, isn't it?

# 14

# The Story Of Good Deeds

A young man who had recently learned the value of good deeds was waiting for an opportunity to do a good deed. He saw an elderly lady on the side of the street who looked like she wanted to cross the street. The young man ran up to her, and holding her hand and arm, he helped her to cross the street. The woman began protesting and beating the young men over the head with her bag.

The young man was surprised and said, "Mother, I am trying to help you cross the street. And now that you have crossed the street, instead of thanking me, this is your behavior."

The woman angrily said, "You fool. I was waiting for my bus across the street, and because you have brought me here, I've missed my bus."

Thus, the young man found out the action he'd thought was so good was, rather, harmful. The only thing the boy could do was to escort the woman back to her original location.

From that day on, he was not in a hurry to do good deeds but thought first about his actions.

At the end of this story, I thought of societies that have created laws to separate human beings. These societies are doing the same thing as the boy. The laws have to do with religion and the unfairness of killings and wars in the name of religion and righteousness and with the sadness of superstitions and close-mindedness. This is especially true of those who think that people of a different faith are filthy, dirty, or physically impure (*najist*), like dogs, which believed to be impure. In case it rains and their clothes and bodies are damp, the so-called faithful must make all precautions to avoid bodily contact with those impures who are not of their religion.

In this modern world, we are still talking about these concepts. Isn't it true to say that there is no difference between one body and another?! The Almighty God that I believe in does not create impurity among his people. These are beliefs that human beings have added to the religion of God. The religion of God is pure. The religion of God is love.

I think the best course of action is to leave the old woman alone and help her only when she asks for help. And I think the best course of action for society is to leave people alone with their ideas and religions and do not force on them ideas they do not want to accept. The religion of God is love.

# 15

# The Story Of Growing Up

It has been many years since I was a child or a young man, when I saw, in my innocent way, this world as complete and perfect.

The world of children is so beautiful that we always try to go back again and become a child once more, far away from this corrupted adult life, where we learn to lie and cheat in order to survive. Accepting adulthood is painful because, despite what we learned during childhood about being honest and good, we have to learn to become crooked and dishonest. Some of us learn to take advantage of others at any given opportunity. The more we learn how to become dishonest to work within the system, to manipulate and lie, and to control our feelings toward others, the easier our lives will become.

Little by little, we learn that many of the most important people in the world, people who are running entire countries, are liars or otherwise lack proper ethics. Little by little, we learn that people who we'd trusted, some very close to us, had lied to us. We learn that many religious people lack ethics and that many who claim to be showing emotions and baring their very souls are not sincere and are deceiving us. Little by little, we learn that, when people tell us they love us, often they do not. Unfortunately, by the time we learn all of these truths, we are already adults. It is too late to deprogram ourselves from childhood's lessons, and we suffer.

Emotion, in its true sense, is the most beautiful thing someone can give us, making at all the worse when it's not real. We learn sometimes not even to trust our spouses, who are our partners for life. What a sad life, and what a shameful world. No wonder we'd like to go back and become children all over again. Isn't it the innocence of childhood that is calling us? No doubt in my mind that is the only reason, "The Innocence".

Like any other child, I thought that all things in this world were in order. By the end of my youth, I learned that the strong always survive, and the weak always get stepped on. The same condition exists in the animal kingdom. The only difference is that, in the animal kingdom, the strong push, bite, and often eat the weak. In the human world, we have reached a point where a stronger creature doesn't eat a weaker creature (even though that remains the case in some parts of the world). However, the physical has changed to emotional, mental, and psychological war. The game has never changed. It is the same barbaric game but played out in a modern fashion. In other parts of the world, almost all of the same conditions exist, but in a so-called politically correct fashion.

One day, in a park where I took my little daughter to play, on the side of the playground these words were written: "The future is at play amongst us." I hope the future that is playing today will have a different world in which to play—a world full of honesty, trust, and fairness to all. I wish for a world just like the world of children, where adults have kept their innocence. That would be the perfect world and it would include no more prophecies, no more messengers, no more waiting for a Messiah.

One day, I am sure, that day will come.

# 16

# The Wrong Attitude

After I finished my education here in the United States, I went back to Iran at the end of 1976. As soon as I arrived, a job was waiting for me with an American pharmaceutical company doing business in Iran. Because of my job, I was privileged to travel all over, visiting major cities of Iran, each more beautiful than the other. From the Caspian Seas and the Azerbaijan states of the north to the Persian Gulf cities and gas-burning pipes in the south. From the Turkish and Iraqi borders to Afghanistan and Pakistan to the East, I was privileged to see them all.

One day when I was in Tehran, my family told me thought I should be working for the government, since I was going to stay in Iran. They made an appointment for to go and see the personnel officer of a sector of a branch of the government. The day came. My aunt accompanied me on my way to see the man. She knew all of these places, streets, every building and every office that we passed.

A security officer accompanied us as we took the elevator and entered a large office. Behind a large and fancy desk, an official received us, and after we were introduced, he told the officer to leave. When I said that I had just returned from the United States, his attitude began to change. I felt he did not like me from that time on. The change might have been a result jealousy of my English-speaking ability or some other unknown reason. He offered me a job out by the Turkish border and said I would have to work a few years there before I would be transferred to Tehran. That was bad enough, but when he told me my starting salary, my blood began to boil. Little by little, my rage started to show. I was thinking to myself, After *all of my education abroad, this stupid man is putting me down like this.*

Before I could open my mouth, my aunt, God bless her, took my arm and pulled me out, asking the man for forgiveness if I had been rude.

As we waited for the elevator, I angrily asked her, "Why did you tell him all of those things?"

She told me to shut up and pulled me into the elevator and then out in the streets.

Once outside she said, "You are crazy. Do you want to disappear? By one call he could have had the security service take you away, and if you find yourself in the hands of the security" (or as they used to call it in those days, the Sovak) "I wouldn't know if you were ever coming back."

Right away, I got the message. For a while, I had been thinking and acting like I was back in America.

I stayed with my job for the rest of my days in Iran. Even there, I was careful, as no one knew who the Sovak members could be. Now, I think the Sovak system was one of the major problems of Iran and one of the causes of the downfall of the Shah. Thank God I am not at all into politics and support no one's side. I am for fairness, freedom for all, and basic human rights. To this day, I remain grateful to my aunt for saving me from those possibilities that could have been very dangerous.

# 17

# What Is The Truth?

I have a friend. His name is Jack. He is an inspiration and is always there for me in good and bad times. His advice is very valuable. One day we were talking about relationships between men and women and how to maintain a good marriage. He told me that a good woman is like a jewel you have to care for very carefully. He said that a bad woman is like a toothache; you need to either pull the tooth out and throw it away or do something about the pain because, if it is not the worst, it will be one of the worse bothering pains. On another occasion, he told me that, wherever you are, you should be like the water in the ocean and flow with the flow of the ocean.

One day I asked him if he knew why we are here—the reason behind the creation. He said that, in the old time, there was a young man who made everybody's lives miserable. He was asking from everybody if they knew the truth behind the creation. He asked so insistently that people could no longer tolerate it. Finally, one of his associates, who was also tired of him asking the same question over and over, told him there was a wise man living on the top of such and such mountain, who was the only one who could answer his question. The young man happily prepared for his journey and began traveling toward the mountain. Day and night he traveled, often without a break, until finally he arrived at the bottom of the high mountain.

He began climbing up, and it took him another day or two before he finally arrived at the top of the mountain. There was a large, flat land that he could see from far away and on it some chickens, sheep, and other animals, as well as a person among them. With lots of excitement, he ran toward the location where he thought the wise man was residing.

When he arrived, after some normal conversation between him and the man on the land, he asked, "Oh, wisest of both universes, what is the truth?"

The wise man looked at him for a while and told him, "Wet birds don't fly at night."

The young man became annoyed and angrily said, "I have traveled day and night to come to see you so that you would tell me what the truth is, and now you are telling me that wet birds don't fly at night."

The wise man looked at him and asked, "Do they?"

The moral of the story is that, in reality, no one knows the absolute truth behind creation. As for those people who claim they know, I feel sorry for them and their ignorance. Unawareness of the truth behind the creation is not only limited to individual human beings; even the worlds religion are limited when it comes to answering this question, as is revealed by the verses of their various texts, which are neither shining nor clear on this point. Scientific theories and concepts also have a long way to go to find out anything about the absolute truth. In the meantime, we are here, and life is too fragile and too short. Why don't we get along, be good to each other, and have wonderful lives?

# The Relativity
# Of Religion

# 18

# My Christian Friend

I have a friend, and we talk a lot, especially about religion and his beliefs and ideas. Here, I try to remember and share some of his views and our discussions. The galore ideas or beliefs that do not make much sense to me. My friend's perspective on people varies according to whether or not they are Christian. He believes all Christians are blessed by accepting Jesus Christ as their Savior. Then he says that Jesus gave his life upon the cross for our sins! When we die, we will be forgiven because Christ paid for our sins with his blood. If any logical person wants to believe all of this, very well. My question is, why don't we commit more sins and do whatever we want, since Jesus has already paid for our sins? Why shouldn't we be responsible for our own actions, instead of Jesus being responsible for them? If we were held responsible for our deeds, wouldn't our sinning be reduced?

My friend believes that, if you are not Christian, you are not going to be saved in the hereafter. Your good deeds, love for humankind, dignity, high moral standards, kindness, decency, brotherhood, and so on will not matter at all if you are not a Christian. Non-Christians will burn in a sizzling fire for all eternity! If you are a Christian, your sins or bad behaviors will be forgiven because you are saved, and somebody already paid for your mistakes.

It is difficult for me to accept that billions of people around the world with different beliefs are going to burn in hell for all eternity just because they are members of a different religion. What kind of a God would be so dispassionate and unjust? How can we possibly square this with our beliefs that God is merciful, kind, and just? This kind of ideology is not limited to Christians. Similar beliefs existed in Islam, as well as in some other religions. In this short life, how many religions do we have to accept in order to not burn in a sizzling hell for all eternity?

Another dread my friend often talks about is the concept of the existence of an almighty devil that he blames for his mistakes or bad behaviors. He says, "It is the work of the devil," or, "The devil made me do it," and so on. These words become as hard as alchemy for me to understand and to digest. I ask him if this is not another way of nonacceptance of responsibility for his actions. "Aren't you blaming someone else for your actions?" I ask. I tell him that possibly the devil is inside his head. He argues that the devil has always existed and will always be there. The story of Lucifer and the time when the devil was actually an angel is another notion in his mind. These words do not make much sense to me.

In my Christian friend's mind, God in the sky or in the garden of heaven has this huge palace, where there are these winged angels flying and implementing the wishes of the Almighty God. This is not only what Christians believe. The exact same beliefs are held by followers of Islam. On the other hand, in both religions as well as all other religions, there are strong statements rejecting or refusing that God has any kind of form or physical body. Also, there are statements rejecting any attributes for God because attributes are conditions of limitation, and God is unlimited and inexplicable. Thus, it becomes difficult to understand the existence of angels and stories of their actions.

Giving the Almighty God a palace just like kings and surrounding it with different angels is only the idea of humankind. God does not have a palace, angels, a crown, or a devil. These are all creations of human beings trying to relate our material world to the world of God. Moreover, scientists indicate that billions of planets exist and that there is a great possibility of life elsewhere beside on earth. So the Almighty God is much greater than what we have in our minds, with his palace, his crown, and his angels running around in heaven. The Almighty God's universe is much bigger than what we can ever imagine.

Nevertheless, we should be thankful for the opportunity of life with all of its experiences, joys, and expectations. We should not wait for God or some magical being to come down and fix our world. We have to fix it ourselves.

Almost all religions tell us that our God is a nonphysical, nonpareil, nonmaterial, and just being—like His universe, an unlimited God. This idea of an unlimited universe, which contains billions of stars and a great possibility of life on other planets, is agreed upon by most if not all scientists. At the same time, this universe is so giant that distances between planets are measured in light-years. Thus during humankind on the earth and perhaps forever traveling or visiting the next planet would be impossible. If the distance between us and the next star is a thousand or even a hundred light years and a person lives at the most one hundred earth years, how can this journey be possible?

This is the size of our God's universe, and the information we have so far might be a very small percentage of all knowledge available. This limited knowledge can provide an idea to the existence of a God who is much more intelligent than the God in holy books, the God that was talking or walking with the man that at one point He created him with His own hands in His image!

We believe that God does not have any physical features. He does not have hands, eyes, legs, a mouth, or other body parts we have. At the same time, we say He *spoke* with such a man or another. If we believe He has no mouth, then how did He speak? And what language did he use? If God is unlimited, then how was He limited to speaking, walking, and having a body?

People of religion always have their own ways. However, is our God limited to talk, or is He unlimited? We cannot have it both ways. God is a creator of billions of planets and not just the planet earth—the planet surrounding Him with all these stories, which are nothing but stories.

It is healthy for us to have some kind of beliefs to help us become better people, but to become extremists and kill people or discriminate against others in the name of God in this extensive universe is wicked, extremely uncivilized, and ungodly.

We as a society or as humankind have to place all religious differences aside and, instead, target problems surrounding poverty and sickness; economic disparity and limits on freedom of choice; environmental degradation; and above all, child abuse.

My Christian friend's mind is limited to this world and only one group of people in this world. The world of God is unlimited, and the people of God's creation are not limited to only one group here. We all are God's children. He views us equally and judges us only by our deeds and not by our religion or beliefs.

# 19

# Religion Or Science

Bernard Shaw, in honoring Albert Einstein, made a famous speech on October 7, 1930, in England at their dinner table. In that speech, Shaw mentioned that religion is always right and protects us from potential problems. Science is always a mistake and can never solve a problem before solving ten other problems. But religion, which as Shaw says is so right, is so full of mysteries that even the scholars in religions are unable to come up with a definitive answer to many questions that a logically minded person can ask. The scholars' answers are usually limited to the "will of God" or the mystery of God and so forth. They say that, where there is faith, there is no logic. The faithful can go places where no logical minded person can go. Then, there is the question of which religion we are going to accept. The number of religions to choose from is unlimited and a confusing issue in its own right.

By looking around ourselves, we can see that there is not just one religion for all of humankind. Rather, there are many religions. Followers of each religion believe that they are the only ones who have the right one.

On the other hand, religion has been the cause of unfairness, killings, and wars—all in the name of righteousness. History is witness that, perhaps, religion has caused more unnecessary killings, bloodshed, and abuses of various kinds than all other causes combined, with the exception of some territorial wars.

If religion, as Bernard Shaw said, is so right and if religion is here for us to be brothers and sisters, what is the reason for all of these killings? Of course, each side in a war has its own reasons. To me, war of any kind is not valid because there is no justice in killing anyone period, beside one of the basic rules of the Ten Commandments is "thou shalt not kill."

We should note that our religion, which is so much a part of us, was chosen for us at birth. Isn't it true that religion is also something geographical? Isn't it true that our parents gave our religion to us at an early age, when we were most ready to adapt beliefs? A person born in China will most likely be a Buddhist; a person born in Israel, a Jewish; a child born in Mexico, a Christian; a person born in Egypt, a Muslim, and on and on. Who is the one to make laws against others, if God is supposedly the ultimate judge?

One might also examine the conflict between science and religion, where science says one thing and religion claims something else. Usually, after a while, religion makes an adjustment to the findings of science. A good example, perhaps, is the work of Galileo, which questioned many churches' beliefs. So a statement such as Bernard Shaw's statement referring to religion and science would be incorrect and damaging to all of the findings of science.

Another example is the argument between science and religion about the theory of creation. The book of Genesis has its own version, and scientists have their own. According to the Old Testament, which is the basis for most non-oriental religions, humanity has existed for five or six thousand years on this planet. According to scientists, existence of humankind on earth can be traced back millions of years.

All in all, though religion has been and remains harmful, we should not forget the contributions religions have made to form order in our society. Otherwise, people would kill each other as they did at the beginning of time.

One cannot overlook the contribution made by science either. Without it, the possibilities of today would remain impossible.

Despite Bernard Shaw's statement, "Science is always mistake," in my view, science, overall, is always right, though it can make mistakes on the way to a final conclusion.

I think it is wrong to compare science with religion or vice versa, even though, for one reason or another, this kind of mind game has existed almost forever.

# 20

# The Fire Worshippers

I was reading a book called *Jewish Religion, History, Ethics, and Culture* by Rabbi Sidney L. Markowitz. It was refreshing to see that the writer, on many occasions, pointed out the long history, involvement, and relationship between Jewish and Persian peoples throughout time. It is important to reveal historical events so they can help us to recover or discover the lost connections between us and help prevent any animosity. It is imperative to remind us of the past and to prevent ignorance, which may exist among some members of each society of this perpetuated Jewish and Persians history.

In chapter three, Rabbi Markowitz mentions the countries that Jewish communities have settled in. The chapter begins, "The history of no country is complete without a consideration of the place of the Jews in that country." The writer names twenty-five countries, and some receive a favorable rating, while others fetch an unfavorable one. Because I do not have knowledge in regard to any of the specified countries, it would be unfair for me to express an opinion or make remarks about them. Examining the parts of history that are gathered in this book for the reader to learn from was a great experience for me. There were points made about the Persians that I did not understand, so I will leave the judgment to my Jewish Iranian brothers and sisters to evaluate the authenticity of the given information.

Rabbi Markowitz writes about the Jews in Iran, "The Jews settled in Persia when Cyrus issued a proclamation restoring Jewish community life in Judea, in the days of Ezra and Nehemiah." He mentions Purim and a duration of one hundred years from 350 to 450 BCE called the "Silent Century," during which, he indicates, the Jews were a numerous and powerful group in Persia. Then he says, "When the fire-worshippers ruled Persia, the Jews rebelled under the leadership of Mar-Zutra. They succeeded in gaining temporary independence for the section where the Jews lived, but the rebellion was crushed and ever since, the Jews in Persia have been oppressed."

It is difficult to understand the meaning of the phrase, "the fire-worshippers" (worshipers was spelled as above) and who it references. If the phrase is referring to the Zoroastrian kings or the Zoroastrians, I do not believe that Zoroastrians are or were ever worshipers of fire. They perhaps used fire to celebrate an occasion or a cultural heritage. Their having gathered around a fire does not mean that they worshiped fire. This is my opinion only. I do not have any documentation or facts to present. However, I found some fragments of history in a book called *Discovering Cyrus* by Reza Zarghamee, in regard to this subject, which I would like to share with you.

We read, "Zoroastrian inspiration for Second Isaiah's revolutionary theology has been claimed on both general and specific grounds. Regarding the former basis, several scholars have observed that Second Isaiah's perception of Yahweh bears a striking resemblance to Ahuramazda, whom Zoroastrians have always venerated as the sole uncreated god." Under the subtitle, "Specific Instances of Possible Iranian Influence," we find, "As Morton Smith has observed, the notion that Yahweh created the world appears sporadically in earlier biblical literature." We also read, "By contrast, the notion serves as a major theme in Second Isaiah's compositions. Specifically the anonymous prophet mentions Yahweh's creation of the cosmos to assure his listeners that their god is powerful enough to repatriate the exiles by manipulating affairs on the world stage, mainly through the actions of his beloved agent, Cyrus. Ezekiel, who lived a generation before Second Isaiah, also foretold the eventual restoration of Israel but without reference to Yahweh's creative powers."

The second point worth mentioning is that the Jews lived in Iran for thousands of years and were always part of Iran from generation to a generation until the tribulations of recent years, which forced many to pack and leave their beloved country.

It is that important to reveal my opinian as I witnessed that no other Iranian ethnics outside Iran has been as effective in preserving the Iranian language, culture, traditions, customs, and way of life in recent decates as the Jewish Iranians. They have demostrate that they truely love Iran and Iran must be proud to raise childern so loyal.

Despite today's apparent in the political arena and the views shared by either sides. This brief may demonstrate a history so pertinent, which could draw a real picture of what has been an indivisible relation during history. A picture which would be different from what is unrealistically evident today.

# 21

# The Stories Of The Bible

I consider myself a religious person who can never deny the existence of the Supreme Being, the Lord God. I wish to believe that, the ethical guideline and moral standards I've followed throughout my lifetime, will ensure that if there is a life after death, I will not be punished forever and ever. One of those standards is to believe in teachings revealed by holy messengers of God from the beginning of the time until today. However, when it comes to many stories in the Bible, especially in the Old Testament, I have no idea what they are saying. As religious scholars, as well as those who are familiar with the stories of the Bible, are aware, the first book of the Bible is called Genesis. Genesis and its stories can be referred to as the foundation of many religions, such as Judaism, Christianity, Islam, and some others. Genesis tells the story of the creation, and it says that approximately five or six thousand years ago, the Lord God came down from heaven or wherever He was residing and, with His own hands, made the first man, called Adam. The Lord God saw that Adam was alone. He created Eve from one of Adam's ribs so that she could be his companion.

The Bible next explains the story of the apple and humankind's first sin. Then there is the story of Cain and Abel, which tells how Cain killed his brother Abel. Cain sorrowfully implicated himself and confessed his sorrow to the Lord God. Thus, sorrowful Cain left his parents' residency, walking and wandering through the fields and the trees. During these wanderings, at an unspecified time of his life, he found a new city, where people were living. Genesis indicates that, Cain decided to stay in this city and take up residency among these other people.

Some questions and predicaments immediately come to one's mind when reading these stories. First, why does this holy book depict killings and sinning from the beginning, instead of showing love and brotherhood?

Second, if there was only Adam and Eve, and they, along with their remaining son Cain, were the only people in the entire world at the time, then who were the other people in the new city Cain found?

In later pages of the old testament we read about the root of the prophecy, and Abraham, whose favorite wife, Sarah, could not give him a son. In order to have a son, he had to marry the maid, Hagar. Hagar conceived and gave a birth to a son named Ismael or Ishmael. After a while, Sarah became pregnant and gave birth to a son named Isaac. Then we read the story of the lamb that was sent to Abraham by God to be sacrificed instead of his son Ishmael, who's blood Abraham was going to be shed for God. Next comes the story of the banishment of Hagar, who was sent away to the east with some water and bread, accompanied by Ishmael. The given reason for this unfairness is that Sarah, Abraham's favorite wife, was jealous of Hagar. I see very little love but unfortunate situations in all of these stories as well.

We read that Isaac became the successor of Abraham, and God gave him two sons, Esau and Jacob. Esau was the older and the favorite son of Isaac. When Esau went out to hunt and gathered food for the family, Jacob stayed home with his mother. Another unjustifiable example appears here when Isaac becomes old and loses his sight. When the time came to introduce his successor, Esau, his choice was absent. His wife, who favored Jacob, used a trick and sent Jacob to be named the rightful successor of Isaac. She cosmetically prepared Jacob to look like Esau, and since Isaac was blind and unaware, he raised Jacob's hand, naming him his successor. Here, we cannot see much honesty, love, or justice either!

Later in the Bible, we read stories relating to King David and his behaviors. One of those stories that is extremely disturbing, if not appalling, tells of a day when, from his window, he saw a woman taking a bath in the river. Though he had many wives and sons and daughters, he sent for the woman, and she was brought to his palace. There, without any guilty feelings, though she was a married woman, he slept with her. David knew she was a married woman and sent her husband to war against the Palestinians, where he could be killed. The result of this affair was a son named Solomon, who became David's successor. The irony of the story is that David had many older sons already, and the oldest son customarily was named successor. If these are men of God, I have to wonder about the men of the devil, in whose existence I do not believe.

The Bible tells many similar stories, which we shall leave them alone. I think that the Almighty God is much greater than all of these stories. He is nothing but love. Besides, a great deal of scientific evidence indicates that our planet earth has been here for many millions of years and dates the existence of humankind here back over millions of years.

As I mentioned at the beginning, I would like to think that I have a profoundly religious acceptance and beliefs. I do not have the power to escape from these beliefs, at the same time I think that reality is different than stories and God is much greater than what we believe. How can we believe that God is only limited to us as most religions are leading us to believe. The earth is flat, at the end of one side is heaven, and at the end of the other is the hell and God is constantly watching us with His inventory list of our good or bad behaviors! There are billions of other galaxies and plants to keep God busy. Why would God keep all these beautiful angels? Are they there to satisfy men with good behaviors? If the answer is yes, what is the difference between that and a prostitution house? As it was questioned and said by Sadegh Hedayat. I do not have the answer to many questions asked, but the only thing that I know the God introduced to us by religions is not the real God if there is One out there.

Moreover, there are always similar ideas and stories from one religion to another. Mithraism worshiped all over Europe for 400 years during the Roman Empire. It ended with Emperor Constantine in 300 AC and replaced with Christianity. Thereafter, it was forbidden to a point that writings, books and their temples were destroyed beyond recognition. However, Mithraism has a root into the Christians beliefs. Here are some examples; The Father, the Holy Spirit and the Son, holiness of number seven, holiness of the sun, Christians changed the resting day to Sunday rather than Saturday, the God's spirit came from the sky and Jesus became the son of God, priests cannot get married, and a whole hosts of beliefs which came from Mithraism to Christianity. Mithraism is pre-Zoroastrian religion, founded in Persia 1500 BC. Another example is that a great portion of the Holy Quran came from the Old Testaments. These stories are the story of Abraham, Isaac, Jacob and Joseph that they all are from the Old Testaments and there are so many verses relating to these stories.

The celebrated Persian poet Rumi who lived 800 years ago said, "I am not from here nor I am not from here nor I am from there. I am not a

Jew, a Christian, nor am I a Muslim…" Perhaps he is trying to say division under any factor is poison to equality and unity. If God is love, why are His religions nothing but love and forced upon people with swords, guns or any mentally abusive systems?

Everything is perfect in His universe, the leaves of trees, the songs of the birds, the light of the moon, the waves of the ocean, and the oxygen we breath to stay alive are all singing songs to us to let us know that there is a God, and God's mercy and love is surrounding us everywhere and every day. And that is the truth.

# The Land Of Freedom And Opportunity, The United States

# 22

# Freedom And Democracy

---

**B**efore we can open this section, it is important to discuss the result of the election in America, which just has been completed in November 9, 2016 briefly. We can see that against the odds and probabilities Mr. Trump wins the election. He does not only desirved to be the president but this process demonstrates the power of the mass in a free world country rather than countries where the result of an election is already decided before the election. The dice falls on the name of a lucky person by one or a group of people where there is no freedom.

It is essential to mention that to demonstrate a free election for self interests, desires or any other reasons would be a refusal of acceptance of "freedom and democracy" in my opinion, eventhough such a right exists. Congratulation to our president-elect Donald Trump, wishing him much success in improving the conditions here in the United States as well as all of humanity in his presidency.

It is also necessary to mention that, the achievements accomplished by president Obama cannot be repudiated. The economy was in disarray, active military personnel lives were in danger abroad, and the world did not have any confidence in US leadership. Mr. Obama restored all of these plus achieving a lot more in a peaceful matter. However, history makes the best judgment of our leaders here in US as well as outside, and my view is irrelevant. Also, history shows a clear picture of each leader of each country as it has done from the beginning of the time.

I remember when Jimmy Carter was running the president of the United States and his historic debate with Gerald Ford. The reporters asked Jimmy Carter if he had any foreign policy experience or if he knew anything about foreign affairs. His favorite work, he replied, was defending human rights around the world, and of course these words were accompanied by his famous smile.

When he became the president of the United States of America one of his first human rights targets was Iran, where allegedly many basic human rights of the civilians were denied and unfairness was institutionalized. It was internationally known that the wealth of the country was in the pockets of a few, and people of Iran were denied freedom of speech.

No attempt was made to promote or improve the tourism industry, to develop historical sites, or to build hotels that would house potential visitors next to these sights. Historical sites are as prolific in Iran as they are in Greece, Turkey, or any area historically belonging to the Romans empire. One such example is the Persepolis, which has a great historical significance, representing a once great civilization that lasted for centuries before and after Alexander. Yet during the Shah's regime, no international promotions enticed visitors to see these monuments. Nor were trained attendants or official groups available to facilitate visits to these miraculous sites. During a time when many nations were building their revenue through tourism, Iran's many wonderful and important sites, with zero international promotion, remained unknown and unused. Perhaps, as happens near other historic sites around the globe, hotels should have been built near these sites to create tourism and accommodate the tourists. Persepolis is like the Colosseum, the Egyptian Pyramids, and other historical sites important to world history. However, it was left as an insignificant pile of rocks, dirt, and stones, alone.

Another source of national pride for Iran are the unique Persian carpets and their outstanding designs, known around the globe. These designs could have been protected, but nothing of the sort was ever done. Consequently, these historical designs with their perpetuating patterns were copied and made elsewhere, by factories rather than hands, and sold much cheaper than the handmade originals were worth.

Despite all of this, the Iranian people were used to the regime, as for the most part, they did not know any better. And those who knew could not talk. On the other hand, people in Iran loved their kings, and they had grown accustomed to the kingdom regimes for over two thousands years. As it is the rule of nature that everything must one day come to an end, the Shah had to go. Primarily because of the influence of foreign forces, his regime collapsed.

President Carter and his human rights policy went to work to crumple the Shah's regime. Carter visited Iran and invited the Shah to visit the United States. I remember that Carter even referred to the Shah as "the island of stability." But as it is known in Iran, also, shared among those who witnessed this process taking place, behind the scenes, forces were to remove the Shah. Though we have to be nice to our leaders and speak nicely about them, here hypocrisy was at its height. The Shah had to go, and he finally left, as this was in the agenda. Of course, these changes were done in the name of democracy and the defense of the human rights.

Despite the policy of the United States, perhaps many other nations were beneficiaries of the removal of the Shah as well. Nevertheless, whether or not the human rights conditions in Iran became better or worse after the Shah's removal was of little importance. What happened in Iran no longer mattered. The job was done.

Exploring further, we can see that, around the middle of April 2015, the Saudi's forces, protected by the United States, opened fire on the people of Yemen, killing innocent civilians and destroying houses, buildings, places of business, and a way of life. The people of Yemen, seeking freedom from a puppet regime, had finally defeated the president and tumbled his regime. The defeated president fled to Saudi Arabia, where he was protected. The Saudis, wanting to refurnish his regime, opened fire on citizens of Yemen to force them to accept the overthrown president.

What a dog-eat-dog world we are living, where people's lives have no value, their desires have no value, and their freedom has no value. I did not hear even a word from an official—not a single senator or member of the House of Representatives spoke up. Nor did any media reporter defend the human rights and freedom of those people dying in Yemen. If the Yemeni people desired a new government and paved the way for this to happen by overthrowing their president that no longer serves them, why are they being bombed? My opinion is not based on my nationality at all. Whenever I see injustice, I write about it. Here, it seems that everything is about the money. The side with the money has the floor, and nothing else matters.

The war in Iraq is another example of this failing idea of protecting the human rights. The human suffering that has resulted from this war is incalculable. How can we impose our desires upon others without a shred of consideration for human life? It can come to mind the semi-secure Iraq of then and the unsettling Iraq of today.

Another example is the changes that have been made in Libya and the overthrowing of the government in that country. I've heard bits about this country in the news here and there, especially in the Senate hearing regarding the Benghazi's incident. But once again, are the people of Libya better off today than they were before outside interference? Is the world safer today or it was safer then?

Another example is the relation with Cuba, which is lasting fifty years. So many attempts were made to kill Fidel Castro as it has been said by the media over and over. However, we do not know who is to blame, Castro's policies or the imposed embargo, which crippled the Cuban economy for this failure that brought poverty to Cuba. Again, for a political reason, people are suffering and they had to find a way to survive among these shortcomings.

It seems to be clear that, to achieve their goals, different administrations in the United States use these wonderful and magical words—*human rights, democracy,* and *freedom.* And when their goals are achieved, whatever happens afterward does not matter whatsoever.

Rather than implementing human rights around the world, instead only talking about doing so is like inviting people to enjoy a smorgasbord of sweet and sour food in a Chinese restaurant where no sweet and sour dishes are served. It appears that plans are to change governments for better or worse in one country today and another country tomorrow. The consequences for the citizens of those countries do not seem to matter, and "protecting human rights" seems only a catchphrase to open a door toward achievement—for better or worse here and there.

At the time, the statement President Carter made about the Shah was a fact. Iran was a major ally of the United States in the Middle East. Many American families were living and working in Iran. I am not certain about the exact number, but it was perhaps between two and ten thousand. And many American companies, such as Johnson and Johnson and others, had manufacturing facilities and employed workers in Iran. Tehran was just like Paris, with young ladies walking around wearing miniskirts. It is not for me to promote any style of dress or dress codes for women or to just go along with women being required to cover up as they are today. Neither do I have any interest in either a Shah-like regime or the current one. I am simply revealing the facts, and it is up to readers to draw conclusions. As most people involved in politics agree, when the Shah was removed from Iran, the entire Middle East was changed forever. Isn't this a fact?

I am not a politician. Therefore, I do not understand what politicians really mean when they talk and use different words in their speeches. When they say something, they really mean something else, and you have to be able to read between the lines. I only understand straightforward, honest talk, without mysteries, hidden agendas, misleading or false promises, or words with double meanings, which are full of hypocrisy.

In conclusions it is necessary to mention that despite all said, "violence is not the answer" and I wish bumper stickers were made and distribute or a campaign would begin here and around the world. By looking at modern history we can see that peaceful people such as Gandhi, Dr. King, and Nelson Mandela were victorious and violent people did not have much success. So, go, "violence is not the answer".

# 23

# "Freedom Was Attacked"

After the tragedy of September 11 in New York, many people's mind traveled to the East. Many understandably differentiated between various sectors and did not rush to make irrational judgments against all people of the East. Various television programs even gave introductions to Islam. Some offered a true picture, and some seemed to fantasize about Islam, rather than acknowledging what Islam really is.

I do not intend to express ideas about the teachings of Islam here. If one has the desire to find out about Islam or any other religion, there are many books written just for that purpose. My writings are about neither Islam nor any other religion.

Religion, though, has been very important throughout history. Its progress has brought hatred, differentiation, separation, and wars. Though the main idea behind all religions is love, sadly enough, we cannot find much love shared between followers of different religions. Even today, after thousands of years, we can see that this idea of religion and love only remains in the holy books, without practice or application. Each religion, with its own sectarian beliefs, claims that its teachings are the best and the only way to salvation. This mix of opposing voices creates confusion and does not offer much love to humankind; rather, it establishes more separation and hatred. Logically, where there are separations and hatred, love cannot be found. Today, each religion continues to preach and to claim that its way is the best way, while there are too many different ways. Thus, existing conditions create conflicts, and where there are conflicts, there will be unsolvable problems, as there are today.

To sit back and wait for a magical holy person, who is called by different names in different religions, to come and fix our conflicts or solve our problems is a waste of time. The magic is life, the air that we breathe, the trees, the mountains, the valleys, and a smile on a child's face. The magic is intelligence, the existence of science, discoveries, research, and the people who are trying to create better living conditions for all of humankind around the world. The magic is funds raised to help individuals and families suffering from tragedies, such as September 11, tsunamis, Katrina, earthquakes, and devastation. We need to work much harder to bring love among humankind and to bring about the "everlasting peace" that God has promised us in every holy book. A Persian proverb describes "a peaceful time, when a lamb drinks water from the same stream, where a wolf drinks."

"Freedom was attacked." These are the exact words used by former President Bush after the September 11 attacks. Now, many years have past, and we can see the outcomes of these words affecting our lives. New laws have been created and imposed on the citizens of the United States in the name of protection. These inconvenient laws are invading people's lives and freedom—the same freedom that was said to have been attacked. Many governmental institutions in the United States, along with their overwhelming costs to taxpayers, came into existence to implement these laws. We went to war, attacked and invaded another nation, and spent trillions of dollars. People were killed, and soldiers gave their lives to show that our government works. All of this was done in the name of freedom— the same freedom that was "attacked."

What is this freedom? What kind of freedom is this freedom? The scholar, Pascal had said that standards change from one geographical area to the next. What is perfectly all right on one side of a mountain could be absolutely wrong on the other side of the same mountain. His statement indicates that freedom has a different meaning in different parts of the world. What is freedom here could be an absolute invasion of a belief on the other side of the world, and what is a freedom there is called, for example, bigamy here. Pornography in the West is considered a freedom of expression. In other parts of the world, pornography is a sinful act and unaccepted. Which is the correct freedom? Each society has its own values, different from those of another. Who is to say which is correct, as each society would insist that their values are superior?

There are other people in the world who have issues far more important than freedom. They need food, clean drinking water, medicine, heating gas, electricity, housing, and so forth. *Freedom* is a fancy word for the poor and economically underserved people who are being suppressed by corrupt governments. It is a definite fact that the majority of people who come to the United States or other wealthy countries do not come to enjoy the freedom but to enjoy the economy and prosperity that do not exist in their own countries. The United States of America consumes a very large percentage of everything produced in the world. Why not join in and prosper rather than stay hungry?

Suppose we took away assets from the people of Glendale and transferred those assets to Hollywood, wouldn't the people of Glendale move to Hollywood in order to enjoy the prosperity there? If we took away their land and homes, wouldn't they become revengeful and terrorists? This is what is happening in our world. We talk about human rights and freedom whenever it serves our interests to do so. And when the interests are met, we forget all about freedom and human rights. We protect kings, heads of state, or presidents of countries who are protecting our interests, though some of those so-call leaders are stealing huge amounts of money from their own people. Go to these countries, and you will see that people are living in very sad, sometimes primitive conditions, often without safe drinking water, electricity, gas, hospitals, and so forth. Wealth from natural resources or other sources goes to the king's bank account, and this can lead to a revolution. Then he brings all the money he has stolen here, which somehow will help our economy. What kind of human rights are these? What is this freedom?

I once read in a magazine that an oil company owns billions or trillions of dollars of gas reserves in an African country. How is it that an American oil company owns reserves worth so much money in a foreign country? How was it paid for and to whom? Isn't it correct to say that those gas reserves belong to the citizens of that country? As I was reading, I remembered the phrase—"freedom was attacked." I read in another magazine that, of every six gallons of gasoline used in the United States, one gallon comes from Mexico. At the same time, I read that the consumption of gasoline in the United States equals the size of the Mississippi River. So, where does the money go, because every time I go to Mexico I see nothing but poverty? The calculation does not add up, and that is how it goes.

The foreign policies of the United States, which have been carried out and are being carried out, are so crucial that they can change people's lives overnight. They can turn historical treasures into piles of dirt in a few days of bombarding. They can make or break a nation in a very short time. However, the American people are the most softhearted, most generous, most affectionate, and kindest people around the world. With all of this money wasted on wars and armaments, we can take care of the education, which in various political arenas there are only talks and not much done about it. And as we are witnessing it has become very expensive and many youths cannot afford it any more.

The global economy depends on a few wealthy nations led by the United States. By various tactics, these wealthy nations monopolize and control the wealth and economy of the world as they desire. Manipulation in governments and sometimes payoffs to the leaders of smaller countries buy these countries' way into the resources of the smaller countries— resources that always generate a tremendous opportunity to gain wealth. Interfering and even invading other countries are pathways to achieving goals. When Manuel Noriega needed to be out, we went and got him, no matter how many solders or civilians were killed. When we needed to remove Saddam, we went and did him in at all costs, no matter how many families were destroyed, how many children lost their parents, how many parents lost their children, or how many soldiers gave their lives. We got Saddam, and that was what mattered. Yes, "freedom was attacked!" What kind of freedom is this?

The visionary messenger John Lennon, in his famous song "Imagine," says, "Imagine there is no country. Imagine all the people of the world, living in harmony." I think, imagining is not good enough any longer. We have to move ahead to the true procurement of the dream. Dr. Martin Luther King Jr., in his famous "I Have a Dream" speech, described his dream. His dream was not just for one sector of our society but for all of humankind. I think we should stop dreaming and move toward the realization and fulfillment of his dream, a dream that would set all of humanity free—free from hatred, intrusion, hypocrisy, lies, separation, and taking advantage of one another. Then, we can thank the Lord and say freedom is here among us at last. We must secure freedom of religion, ideology, culture, race, and belief around the world with a real intent. Then we can see a lamb drinking from the same stream where a wolf is drinking. Then we can say freedom is here among us, at last, at last, and at last.

# 24

# Happy Father's Day

I do not know whether we should credit women for their cleverness or blame men for being so preoccupied by their occupations, thus becoming unimportant members of their families, especially in the United States. Of course, to me mother is a very special person, and it is important to recognize the station of motherhood, which without a doubt, is and has always been the most loved station. A mother deserves all the levels of love that she receives. Nevertheless, up to recent years, fatherhood had also a special station, and fathers played a big role in bringing up children. Fatherhood was the authoritative station. To prove my point, we can refer to the Old Testament, the New Testament, the Koran, or any historical book to see that, for thousands of years, man had the power, and that was the way it was. By a series of laws and social attitudes, little by little, fatherhood has been diminished, until today, we see fathers portrayed as sometimes useless, less smart than mothers, or lacking authority. Maybe some of the social problems of today's complex lifestyle can be traced to this reason and these changes.

The inspiration for what I am trying to say is an article printed in the *Los Angeles Times* on June 18, 2000, written by Roy Rivenburg. The article was a source of good laughter for my wife and me. She loved it, and I was kind of appalled by it. The title of the article was "It's Dad's Day (but Mom Still Wears the Pants)." The date and the title make it clear that the article's subject is Father's Day. Mr. Rivenburg gives a history of Congress' official establishment Mother's Day and Father's Day to honor Mom and Dad in the United States.

Here are some or the statistical differences between the two days. Referring to the days in a one-year period, we can see that Mother's Day is ahead, and in any given year, it comes first. Mr. Rivenburg's indications are self-explanatory:

a) Phone calls – On Mother's Day, 155 million calls Army, compared to Father's Day, at 140 million calls. More collect calls are made on Father's Day than on any other day.

b) Greeting card sales-Mother's Day sees the purchase of 150 million cards, while for Father's Day, 95 million cards are bought.

c) Dining out-On Mother's Day, 38 percent of adults eat out. On Father's Day, 23 percent of adults eat out. Mother's Day even tops Valentine's Day for restaurant dining.

d) Top gifts-Clothing tops the list of Mother's Day, while neckties are number one on Father's Day.

e) Flowers-Mother's Day accounts for 23 percent of all holiday floral sales. Father's Day isn't even on the chart. Men are statistically more likely to get flowers at their funeral than for Father's Day.

So, here we are. Who would think that fathers would not like to receive flowers or at least equal treatment on their designated day? Of course, discussion here is about those fathers who accepted their responsibilities side by side with mothers and worked to bring up their children to the best of their abilities. We are not concerned about those who actually were not fathers by not accepting their responsibilities for any reason.

Finally, I am not discrediting those mothers who are forced to play the roles of both mother and a father under extremely difficult circumstances. Rather than basketball or football players, movie stars, or any other celebrated personalities, those mothers should be recognized as the heroes of society.

# 25

# In Courtrooms

The main objective of having laws is to protect society and its people. This concept is honorable but often broken, to a point that people have to protect themselves from the laws. We can see that, often, someone who is guilty of a crime is found not guilty, while someone else who is innocent is found guilty. People who are rich can buy the law by hiring the best lawyer or a team of lawyers able to manipulate the law to the advantage of their clients. This very setup goes against justice and fairness for all. Poor people are incarcerated for any number of minor misbehaviors, while white-collar criminals are not even indictable.

Court processing is a long, nerve-racking process, where a strong person with money often survives and a weak person without money is quickly demolished. Often it is an unfair battle between the rich and the poor, leaving lawyers, judges and others who takes advantage of the miserable system the only beneficiaries—all obtaining excellent benefits.

There operation of the court systems involves massive waste. Though we need laws and we need people to obey the laws and to try to make the laws work, often enforcing the law become abusive and a waste of time, energy, and money and sometimes killing inocent people on the streets by the police. Maybe that is how the law and the courts are supposed to work, for the poor and rich. Some laws are set to protect other laws, instead of protecting people. Some laws are so complicated you have to have a degree in law to understand what they mean. One can ask whether the law serves to protect us or whether we have to protect ourselves from the law.

In the end, you can't help but thinking it's all about the money. As the old song says, "The man gets caught with twenty kilos serves no time," but a little guy with an ounce on the street keeps going in and out, "and that's the way it goes." I am not talking about the losing war on drugs, the channel of distribution, who is involved with it, and who is actually benefit from it. I'm not addressing these issues because I have no idea what goes on, but I can imagine that, one way or another, drug trade has impact on the economy. I am only referring to it to demonstrate how the laws are working. This failure and decay of our system has been around from the time of Al Capone.

In the United States, it seems that too much power has been given to the judges without check and balances of their rulings. One judge says something, and a few months later, another judge says the exact opposite.

Judges often issue unfair, unjust, harmful, and even ridiculous and torturous rulings. Two cases may be indicative of how dangerous society can become under these kinds of rulings. The first example was a story I heard on a radio talk show. A judge obligated a husband to pay child support to his ex-wife for children from her previous marriage. In other words, if a man marries a woman with a child or children, he will become automatically financially responsible for those children. I am not a sociologist, but one can imagine the negative impact on women with children. What man in his right mind would accept such a difficult task? Of course to some people, the answer is the man who is in love, and I have no problem with that. Generally, it seems that this ruling is far away from fair to either gender. Hopefully, the judge himself becomes part of his own law.

The second example is even more unjustifiable. A married woman committed adultery and become pregnant with the adulterer's child. At the divorce proceedings, the judge ordered her husband to pay years of child support for a child who was not even his. This child was a product of an adulterous affair. What does the child have to do with the husband? Isn't the real father responsible for his child? Instead of being forced to take responsibility for one's actions, the adulteress received a reward. What is wrong with our world? The judge's cited reason for his ruling was the probable difficulty of finding the real father. Therefore, he ruled, the husband must provide for the child. My answer to the judge would be that he himself should pay for the child support if he was so concerned about the child's affairs. After all, the judge most likely is making more money than the poor husband. Moreover, isn't the husband already crushed by his wife's behavior? Why is the court torturing him more? No wonder the world is full of so much crime and so many crazy people.

A while back, with the Rampart Police Department scandal in Los Angeles, people became more aware and informed about the dirty jobs police officers sometimes do. We see that police officers are not all clean like they are supposed to be. Some officers had been framing people; they'd lied in the court and planted evidence to get convictions. The police corruption is not limited to Rampart or to the police officer/rapist in Lafayette, Louisiana, who, for ten years, terrorized people. He had access to the investigator's data and, therefore, was able to avoid detection. Another example was in Chicago, and another happened in New York. John Orr in Glendale committed arson. And the list can go all the way to the Mafia mobs or before. Although the majority of those who are to be trusted with our lives and belongings have done remarkable jobs, some have done dirty work, embarrassing the police force.

However, when police officers lock someone up, wrong or right, that person will be marked for rest of his or her life. Therefore, we can see that, to have any kind of engagement with police can result in never-ending consequences. For this reason, its best to walk a fine line so we do not have to pay for life with our dignity.

It is evident that even presidential candidates will face embarrassing moments for something they have done twenty years earlier. Something that happened within a completely different context than of today can resurface and reflect a character now. People's files are open until death and beyond, even if they are wrongfully convicted. The system is not very concerned with a person's good deeds but, rather, focuses primarily on bad deeds.

Perhaps, people with good behaviors, after a certain time, could be forgiven and could have a new start. The Department of Motor Vehicles provides an excellent example of how that could work. With the DMV's system, after three or five years, a person's negative points disappear. The credit system, which allows people's credit to be reestablished after so many years, is another example the criminal system might follow. If incarcerated, hardened criminals serve less time with good behavior, then why can't we wash peoples' records, as if their crimes never happened and give them a hope for a future?

I think branding people as criminals for all of their lives will not help anyone, and these labels should be cleared, except for in the cases of hardened criminals such as child molesters, multiple rapists, murderers, and people who are dangerous to society. Perhaps, some hardened criminals, after a certain time, could be forgiven, so they could have a chance to become productive citizens. Whether or not someone wants to be a good citizen all depends on his or her behavior.

It would cost twenty or thirty thousand dollars a year to provide for an inmate. US government spends about forty billion dollars a year to incarcerate the criminals. Perhaps, the money spend for the same cause at the state, city, and local levels rivals the same amount if it is not greater. If more money was spent for education, there were no need to spend so much to incarcerate people. As doctors say "prevention is always the best solution". We keep people like Charles Manson around for years to learn from them, what is it that we have learned?

# 26

# Promises of Politicians

In this divided world, one day there is a bombing in Paris, one in Brussels on another, one in Turkey on still another, and one in Pakistan on the next. Here, there is an attack on the world's trade center one day, and a Russian plane is downed on another. All these are examples of how the way of life has been changed around the world. The politicians had promised us that, by changing various regimes, the world would become a better place, mainly for the people of those countries in which the regime change took place. In reality, the world has become a worse place ever since these changes began taking place. It would be difficult for me to say whether changing the Shah of Iran and the establishment of an Islamic state for the first time was the turning point or the downfall of Saddam Hussein's regime or the disassemblage of Gaddafi from Libya or all of the above. According to the administrations involved in them, these changes were vital, so much so that, in one instance, American lives were lost to achieve the goal, though, unfortunately, in vain. Nevertheless, the politicians keep on promising.

During my lifetime, I have come to the conclusion that politicians or those who run governments have, from the beginning of time, often made empty promises. They often say one thing but actually mean something else. Though a policy seems to be working for the public, they will change it around, and soon it will not work. One day, some kind of social program will be on their agenda, and a few years later, that same program will have become a bad idea. One day, building up a military force is on their agenda, and a few years later, building such a force would be a waste of energy and money (which is actually true).

Even the communist ideology, after having been a huge force for many decades, suddenly seems like it's not working. One day, the capitalistic ideal will be the absolute system of government, and later, it will become obsolete. Under this ideal, society is not running fairly. The resources become the property of the rich, and thus, the rich become richer, while the poor get poorer. The kingdom methods, which for millenniums were the only system of governing, do not work anymore because kings were the absolute power and often the wealth of nations belonged to them.

One day, religion will combine with governments, creating an absolute dictatorship by enforcing laws in a certain holy book, many of which, in truth, come from humankind rather than a holy source. Thus, this system will become abusive and dangerous. Even when churches and governments are separated, we can still see religious concepts influencing policies. That is how the politicians run things.

Some governments try to help people by imposing heavier taxes to reduce the consumption of a product that is harmful to the public. An excellent example is the tax on cigarettes; the average cost per pack in California is approximately five dollars. This amount consists of the manufacturing and production costs, the wholesaler and retailer's profit, and the imposed taxes. While reducing smoking is an excellent idea, in truth, many of those who want to smoke continue to do so, and the money they spend on cigarettes may take away from funds for their family's food or other needs. Unless the government makes it unlawful to smoke, which is the only solution, people will smoke.

Another example is the politicians' promise of the California Lottery. At its conception, the lottery was introduced for a good cause, which was an additional source of income for education and schools. Soon after, politicians determined the average income per a certain time, and they took away the same amount from the education budget, leaving the budget with a net zero from the lottery income. Come to think of it, one cannot imagine how much income Los Angeles County and the state of California receive daily, monthly, or annually by collecting property taxes on millions of houses; those from commercial, agricultural, and residential lands; and registration fees, business permits, and so on.

The US Constitution is not a source of pride exclusively for citizens of the United States; around the world, people cherish its values. Under this Constitution and the freedoms enjoyed in the United States, the nation has sent men to the moon. I was very young when my father and I cried for joy to witness such an achievement. Things have changed from then. No longer does the United States measure up to the "perfect, ideal society" of Thomas More.

Dr. Martin Luther King, in his speech made in Riverside, New York, opposing the war in Vietnam said, "Silence is the sign of a perpetrator." As I do not wish to be a perpetrator, then I need to say what I think it would breack discriminations and bring equality to all of humanity. Certainly, my words will never measure up with those of Dr. King, but I think everybody has a responsibility to say what he or she is thinking.

The gap between the rich and the poor has become wider now than ever before. The minimum wage increase in a long run has always worked against the poor, disabling them and preventing them from affording higher prices brought on by the inflation resulting from the wage increase. I think the percentage of inflation followed by a minimum wage increase would be always higher than the minimum wage itself.

There are no specific agendas designed at the city, state, or federal level to address the homeless problem. Homeless citizens are left on the streets by the hundreds, relying on churches or privately owned institutions to care for them. The question that comes to mind is, how is it that the United States can go all over the world interfering with other nations' affairs but cannot solve its own problems?

Of course, for some homeless, a monthly check is issued by the government, but a check is not a solution. There are no systems of monitoring at various governmental levels to provide assurances of improving the condition of homelessness. The government has not dealt with the problem of drugs and the homeless. Instead, that can has been kicked to the side. Perhaps the government could introduce a program wherein a homeless person is brought back into the workforce in a factory or on an agriculture field in order to receive a paycheck or a program that would eventually place a homeless person into the workforce. Something needs to be done, rather than leaving masses of homeless people on the streets. Go and see the east side of downtown Los Angeles at nights to understand this predicament. There are clinics supposedly providing services to stop addiction. However, a drug addict can go into this kind of institutions for years without any result. Most likely, many addicts go there just to obtain whatever amount of drug they can get.

No monitoring systems document the rates of success or failure among these clinics either.

California ranks number 6 and becomes one of the world's largest economy passing France and Brazil in 2016. Gross national income of Brazil is approximately 2.9 trillion dollars a year. With this kind of economy power, drought is still a major problem shared by individuals, agricultural fields, and industrial zones in California. Ocean is an unlimited source of water. How is it that billions of dollars spent on making jet bombers by the government and no dollar is designated to convert the ocean's water and give it to people to use it rather than limiting their conceptions as well as rising the price of water usage? It does not seem to have any plans at the state or federal levels to address this problem and its solution.

The economic gap between the poor and the rich has become wider now than ever before. I suggest that anyone who disagrees first go see the mansions in Bel Air or Beverly Hills and then pay a visit to Century Boulevard and Broadway, west of Watts or parts of the Athens, and south of Los Angeles to compare the life conditions in both places. Then, he or she can make a reasonable conclusion as to whether, in this society, justice for all or fairness was ever considered. Perhaps, instead of simply building freeways that pass through these kinds of stressed neighborhoods, we should build universities and technology centers, as well as centers designed to spur the economy and improve residents' life conditions. Otherwise the ghetto will always be the ghetto, and the hood will always remain the hood.

Yes, politicians promise a lot, and they sometimes harm instead of help.

# 27

# Racism

Racism plays a big role in people's life. It appears differently in different parts of the world. In one society, racism looks at skin color, as seen in the United States of America still today. Given the overwhelming prevalence of racism in one of the most advancred countries of the world, one can imagine the terrible conditions that exist in other parts of the world. In some societies, racism is in the form of bigotry. People of religions other than that practiced by a ruling government are foredoomed to be killed or imprisoned without reasons. These people are often robbed by mobs without protection from authorities. To have a different religion or simply to not have one becomes an unjustifiable crime, punishable by death. Ethnicity, gender, and variations or combinations of different sources of bigotry can be created in some societies in order to achieve goals.

Racism and bigotry have brought too many sad conditions around the world at different times in history. My hope as I write about this subject is that, one day, all stereotypes, racism, and prejudices will disappear forever from all corners of this beloved world and people will live in peace and love as promised by God in the holy books.

Right or wrong, these are my perceptions, which I've gained through a lifetime of experience about sectors I've had the pleasure to be in contact with. I am referring to general cases, and as we know, there are exceptions to any rule. So, without further delay here is my view about various people.

Points about Iranian people (my own nationality)

Iranians are introduced to the world as bomb-carrying terrorists and uncivilized people. The average Iranian is hospitable, sharing, warm, intelligent, informed, eager to help, and kind. They also have lots of artistic and poetic abilities. Storytelling is a cherished Iranian ability, reflected in tales from *one thousand and one night* which includes the stories of "Aladdin and the Wonderful Lamp," "Sinbad the Sailor," and hundreds of other volumes. Iran has played a large part in the world's civilization. Despite today's appearances, freedom, which seems to be a product of the Western world, was originated five centuries BC in Iran, as we know, by Cyrus The Great.

*Their negative points-* Iranians can be opportunistic, greedy, and gold diggers. Some speak straightforwardly, while many do not. Some are aggressive and arrogant, unable to promote internationally their heritage and contributions to civilization. Racism and discrimination against believers of religions other than Islam are highly prevalent, despite the Tablet of Freedom written by Cyrus the Great. Rather than minding their own business, many Iranians make too many disturbing, invalid comments about Jewish people and Israel, though Iran has a long history of ties with the Jews, all the way to Esther and to Cyrus. Iranians in recent years are too wrapped up in religion, instead of focusing on their economy and making advancements in agriculture, manufacturing, technology, and science. It is a shame that, with all the natural resources Iran has, the nation is placed behind some neighboring countries, which are much smaller and lack Iran's wealth of resources.

## Points on Jewish people

Many Jewish people are sharp, informed, intelligent, business-minded, good-hearted bargainers, who measure the value of their work by the quantity of their earnings. Many are good storytellers, innovators, oriented by science, politically aware, convincing communicators, and excellent investment planners.

*Their negative points-*Greedy, calculative, stingy, trusting only their own, and far too proud of their heritage, Jewish people drag around things from decades or centuries ago, instead of letting bygones be bygones. Take for example, all the movies are made and are still making by mostly Jewish producers about the Holocaust. Of course, Hitler's actions were horrible and a shame to human history.

Nevertheless, every nation has some kind of genocide in its history, and the Persians are probably the greatest example. First, Alexander burned their civilization. Then there was the attack of the Arabs. Next came the Mongols, whose horrible actions against the Persians are documented in history. We do not see the Persians making movies about these horrible massacres that occurred over and over throughout history.

Another example of human massacre and suffering is that of the American Indians, another is that of the Armenians, and yet another is that of the Philippines. The list goes on and on. Thereby, taking measures to stop such occurrences is essential, so that humankind does not encounter these tragedies again.

It is also difficult for me to agree that the Jews are the chosen race by God, as the God I believe in does not discriminate. We all are the children of God. One is white, one is black, one is brown, and one is yellow. It is difficult to accept that God would choose one group of people over others. If God does this, then how can we accept that He is a just God? We all are His children, with equal treatment and punishment.

## Points on Latinos

Many Latinos are humble, often tranquil, happy to spend, and sincere. As a whole, they are great producers, cooperative, and fun-loving people who let the good times roll. Actually, in my experience the Latinos, except for the European Latinos (since I have had no contact with them) could be classified in two or three different groups—(a) those from Mexico and some parts of Central America, (b) those from Central America and parts of South America, and (c) the South Americans. As we go from the north to the south, the level of sophistication rises, as does arrogance. The people from Argentina, Chile, and Uruguay are somewhat different from the people of Mexico. So it is difficult to generalize about Latinos. However, the majority of characteristics mentioned above would apply to all Latinos. Most Latinos are hardworking people, and they are very important to the economy of the United States.

*Their negative points*-Many Latinos are humble to the point that other ethnic groups take advantage of them. Many of their children grow up in the United States and get involved with drugs and gang activities. Teenage pregnancy and high birth rates are leaving too many in poverty. Some Latinos do not focus much on education but on drinking and sexual activities. A man with a wife and five children may leave for a different wife or vice verse. Of course, such behavior is not limited to Latinos only.

## Points on black people

Though they are known as being brutal, heartless, and angry people, the average black person is kind, funny, amusing, and full of good humor. They are respectful citizens full of artistic abilities, athletic ability, and energy. They are easily pleased and thankful. They are very proud, politically aware, intelligent, and aware of civil rights.

*Their negative points*-Black people, just like the Jewish people, drag behind them things from the past, instead of letting go. They watch out for their own race instead of humankind. Some may sell you short, and some are after easy money. Limited black youths' criminal actions give black communities a bad name. Addressing the subject of race around them becomes complex to a point where it becomes difficult to talk about it at all.

For example, Charity Jackson became like my mother in the United States. However, being around her, I became uncomfortable when we talked about racism. Sometimes she would make me something to eat, and sometimes I would take her out. Before she passed away, we traveled together to Mexico a few times, sometimes going as far as Ensenada. In each other's company, whether we were traveling or just hanging out, we often talked about everything, but even with her, I was not comfortable discussing the simple subject of racism.

## Points on white people

Many white people are smart, helpful, kind, and generous. They are educated, technologically aware, good moneymakers, and career orientated. Planning and investing skills, self-confidence, and lack of shyness make them good communicators. They are often skilled at convincing others of their point of view.

*Their negative points*-White people can be manipulative, and they like to dictate to others their point of view. Some are jumpy and get angry quickly. Some want to know everything about you, asking too many questions. Many are looking for easy money. Some are demanding and have unreasonable expectations of others. They do not believe other people are as smart or as deserving as them.

It is true that racism is a joke, but it is a kind of joke that no one can laugh about. It has become a very sensitive issue because of an unreasonable fear within our society. Consequently, we all try to cover up our racist feelings.

To clarify what I mean, I refer to the following story I once heard. Two ladies were having a discussion in the hallway of their workplace. The topic of discussion was black peoples' use of the "n word" among themselves and how nobody complains about it, but as soon as people of other races use the same word, it becomes a big deal. Two black women were listening to this conversation from a distance, and one can imagine the rest of the story. I was not there to make a judgment about whether or not the ladies' statement were designed to be racist and, if so, whether they deserved to receive what they got. If not, a punishment would not be fair.

It would probably be a lie for anybody to say that he or she is never racist or at least never experiences some kind of latent feeling toward a given group of people. To be polite or politically correct, we hide our feelings, and that creates a dangerous or unhealthy condition for all. If we do not change the conditions, how are we going to stop racism? If racism is a joke, then why can't we joke about it and have a good time with it? If it is not a joke, then we should take it seriously and respect each other for whatever and whoever we are.

As for societies that are extremely uptight, close, or dark-minded when it comes to tolerating other religions, those societies need to relax and allow their people freedom of choice. As is said by all religions' leaders, there are thousands of ways to reach God. Thus, every man and woman is entitled to his or her choice. Who are we to play God?

# 28

# Same Places, Same People, Different Names

There was a big problem for me, and I am certain that it is shared among millions of people from different parts of the world who are living in the United States or other English-speaking countries. I am referring to the problem of English nomenclature when it comes to "translating" foreign names. While some names remain the same, or almost the same, others are quite different from their origins when translated to English. For example, names such as Ali, Buddha, Miriam, Tokyo, Washington, and Quito are the same in English as in their languages or origin. On the other hand, names such as Moses, Jesus, Cyrus, Egypt, Germany, and Cairo have different names in different languages.

I hope this discussion will focus attention onto the global discomfort caused by this issue. In order for the issue to garner the attention it merits, it is important to achieve universal awareness of this existing dilemma. Maybe then, in some form or another, corrections will be made to standardize all names and eliminate this international predicament and confusion.

Perhaps, the original pronunciation of names-in their language of origin-should be considered correct and should not be changed. This would avoid the misunderstanding and confusion that results from different forms being used to refer to the same persons or places. For example, these names, given first in English and then in their Farsi equivalent—Cyrus (Kuroush), Darius (Dariush), Xerxes (Khashayar), Pharaoh (Ferown), Egypt (Masr or Mesr), Ethiopia (habasheh), and Greece (Younoun). Though each pair of names is used to refer to the same persons or places, they look and sound completely different from one another, which is confusing. I have given examples in Farsi and in English, as those are the ones above. But perhaps every language has its share of the same confusion. When I was learning English, this issue made it impossible for me to connect the knowledge I'd learned in Farsi to the same knowledge in English, creating massive misunderstandings and difficulties, to the point that I did not know who was who and what was what.

As mentioned earlier, an examination of a smattering of names that have crossed into one language from another makes it clear that some names have received minor or no changes, while others have completely changed, creating confusion and difficulties. It is difficult to understand why such changes came to be and who caused them. In one language, Egypt is called Egypt, while in another language, Egypt is called Mesr.

Perhaps, one of the most misspelled, misrepresented names in the world is the name "Iran." Though I grew up to love the name, Iran as is spelled in English does not represent what the name was originally changed to mean. The reason the ancient name *Persia* was changed to the modern *Iran* is because it has come to light that, at the beginning of the second millennium BCE, the ancestors of the Aryans settled in the land today called Iran. The Aryans were a broad population, including the Medes and the Persians. Tribes each occupied a different part of Iran. Thus, the name Iran was adopted to signify and represent the land that was occupied by the Aryans. Though in Farsi's spelling, this representation is visible, the way it has been spelled in English does not allow for this significance to be visible. Consider that France is where the French people live, England is where the English people live, China is where the Chinese live, and so on. The name Iran is supposedly designation where the Aryan people live. If that is the case, then the spelling of the English version should reflect the intent; it could be Aran or Aryan or some other form, but not Iran. Iran to me, as well to millions of other people around the world, as is spelled in English in no way signifies "the homeland of the Aryan."

Going back to the subject of changing names, I think it is essential to have a clear mind of pronunciation of names wherever we may travel because names have different forms in different parts of the world. It is important to understand and know what a person you're communicating with is referring to, as communication is the gateway of understanding. It is difficult to translate or transmit the phonics of a language into another language. Therefore, minor differences in pronunciation or spelling are acceptable. But to change the form of a name completely is a bad idea, perhaps with bad intent.

Here is a brief English and Farsi comparison of some name of places and persons:

a)  Persons

| | | |
|---|---|---|
| Aaron | = | Haroun (brother of Moses) |
| Abel | = | Habil |
| Achaemenids | = | Hakhamanishian |
| Alexander | = | Eskandar |
| Avicena | = | Ibn-e-Sina (the father of medicine) |
| Caesar | = | Qyesaar or Qaesar or Ghaesar |
| Caín | = | Qabel or Ghabil |
| Christ | = | Masseah |
| Cyrus | = | Kuroush |
| Darius | = | Daryush |
| Eve | = | Hava |
| Gabriel | = | Jebrail |
| George | = | Jirjiss |
| Ghaznavids | = | Ghaznavian |
| Hagar | = | Hajar |
| Herod | = | Herodus |
| Isaac | = | Es-hagh or Es-haq |
| Ishmael | = | Esmail |
| Jacob | = | Yaghoub |
| Jehovah | = | Yehovah (title of God in Hebrew) |
| Plato | = | Aflatoon |
| Seljuks | = | Saljukhian |
| Sheba | = | Saba |
| Tamerlane | = | Temur-e-lang |

b) Places:

| | | |
|---|---|---|
| Austria | = | Otrish |
| Cairo | = | Qahereh or Ghahera |
| China | = | Cheen |
| Cyprus | = | Qebres or Ghebres |
| Egypt | = | Masr or Mesr |
| Ethiopia | = | Habasheh |
| Greece | = | Younoun |
| Georgia | = | Gorgestan |
| India | = | Hindostan |
| Jerusalem | = | Orshaleem |
| Jordan | = | Ordun |
| Palestine | = | Philestin or Filestin |
| Poland | = | Lahestan |
| Russia | = | Ruseeyh |
| Switzerland | = | Swiss |

The above list is not complete. Rather, it is only an example to show the existence of this global complication, which an English-speaking person may or may not be aware of.

The above illustration included mostly Farsi pronunciations, as well as some Arabic and Hebrew. I have tried to approximate the spelling as close to the sound as possible. Consequently, my spellings may vary from others, as there are various ways to spell foreign names in English.

# 29

# The Economic Machine

Ever since the civil rights movement of the 1960s, led by men like Malcolm X and Martin Luther King Jr. to provide basic freedom to black citizens in the United States, a new chapter has been added to an old subject in our history book—that of human dignity, human rights, and freedom. The history book began a little over 2,500 years ago with Cyrus the Great, who freed the Jews from captivity.

The subject of economy is informative and interesting. It shows who is benefiting and who is losing in any given society. In some societies, members of governing bodies with their friends are the beneficiaries for stealing and the average public are the losers because there is nothing left for them to live on. The governing members take advantage from their opportunity to get rich quick because they are dishonest and do not care for their countries nor for its citizens. In the United States, there are two complete different schools of thought in economy and in governing policies. One school is for limiting the size of government; maintaining lower tax and empowering the business communities. The second school is for expenditure of the size of government through social assistance, welfare, Medicare for all as well as other public services. The second school requires a higher tax bracket applied one way or another. I am not going to select one method over another but to point out only that the US debt is growing at the highest speed in history, which is not sustainable. The US owes more money than any country in the world and it is unlike the US that I know and remember. As of today, May 15, 2023 the debt accumulated to 31.46 trillion dollars. A trillion is one with twelve zero after it. The interest payment alone in fiscal year 2022 was 475 billion dollars, which is an astonishing figure.

Here are some wasteful spending habits, which never monetized to evaluate their results. First is the incarceration method and treatment of people so called "criminals". It is shameful for the most advanced nation in the world to have such a current corrupted system. Billions of dollars spent each year for room and board and other needs of inmates without any ending positive results. Instead of helping prisoners through education to better their lives and to better the society, it has become a bullying place where inmates are often abused physically, mentally or sexually creating a chain of violence throughout the society. How can a person become a better person in such an abusive environment? There should be educational programs, where a new comer can sign up to become a carpenter, electrician, mechanic, accountant, computer programmer, nurse and so forth at arrival. It would enable them to provide for themselves after release to become a productive member. There should be mandatory blood test upon arrival isolating substance abusers to rehab centers where they can become clean then sign them to a career-training program. There should be trained officers who do not accept bribe money prevent violence at spot rather than promoting and focusing only on education of inmates. This is one way that we can be proud of our nation, which can be an example to follow.

Second, wasteful program without accountability is dealing with social programs such as food stamps, Medicare for all, rental assistance, welfare and so on. The existing method does not offer a long-term solution but it is only an easy fix kicking the can down the road. There should be again carrier-training centers educating people to go back to work. Addiction is one of the most setbacks of societies and an advance nation like the United States should not procrastinate but deal with this nationwide problem. There should be rehab centers in all largest cities providing rehabilitation to those who are involved with this disastrous habit to overcome this distorting social obstacle. These kinds of assistances would eventually bring more tax to help the government.

Defense budget has lots of wastefulness that we have all heard different stories that there is not accountability and control over purchasing. Another example is a $ 75 billion directed to Ukraine since the war began, which is greater assistance than all European nations combined that are directly involved and closer to Ukraine than is the United States. This money has to be borrowed with interest payments to the US spending abroad rather than inside the country! Renovation must take place to correct this wasteful method and culture in every department and if people cannot be trusted with money, the new AI technology is the solution.

Cyrus established freedom as a basic human right, as has been captured in various documents, such as the Cyrus Cylinder and other ordinances. It is important to note that our civilization began with Cyrus, who brought order and a governmental idea into the society of humankind for the first time. Though there were kings and governing forces before Cyrus, such forces were limited to localities and smaller areas. Cyrus changed the system of governance. He conquered and ruled over the largest geographical area of the time. He offered freedom to all different cultures and beliefs under his realm. After Cyrus, for various reasons freedom vanished in different places and times throughout the existence of humanity. Sometimes this freedom was taken away because of a dictator and sometimes because of a new conqueror and some time because of existing ideologies in a religion.

As different religions came into existence, the mind game and struggle between various humanity began. Some religions even used deadly force to defend their beliefs—though most religions claim that God is love and religion's goal is to bring brother and sisterhood among men and women. A great example of using deadly force can be the 11th, 12th, and the 13th centuries Crusades between Christians and the Muslims over position of the Holy Land.

That is how things were until the modern era, which produced many powerful demonstrations, the beginnings of which can be traced to the most dominating, peaceful demonstration in India, led by Mahatma Gandhi. Gandhi was a man of honesty, honor, and extreme peace. His demonstration was about how and why Great Britain was taking India's raw materials without making any payment or sufficient payments. This nonviolent fight continued even after Gandhi was gunned down and killed, until the day that finally the Great Britain was forced to begin making payments.

One of the most significant documents providing freedom in modern history is the Constitution of the United States of America. However, the Constitution provided a guideline and an ultimate ideological method to follow. The civil rights movement of the 1960s breathed life into an idea born in the Constitution. The civil rights movement was organized essentially to guarantee freedom and better living conditions for black people living in the United States of America. Though Dr. King was also against violence, many walks and demonstrations ended violently when Dr. King was also eventually gunned down and killed. All in all, black citizens of the United States made their points, and the American public was brought to accept their demands that would guarantee their freedom. Many talents have appeared ever since and every day as a result of this change. This demonstrates that no man or woman is better and no man or woman is worse but that all humankind are created equal.

Yes, blacks people in the United States are free, but what is the meaning of freedom of flying when you do not have enough money to buy a plane ticket? What is the meaning of freedom when your legs are tied down to an economic machine that does not allow you to walk? Today, the vast majority of black Americans lives in areas of cities across the United States that lack economic movement. Busing children from places like Watts or Compton to Beverly Hills does not solve any problems but could add to them. Wouldn't it better to change the living conditions in places like Watts to make it comparable with Beverly Hills?

The economic machine has to stop at the ghetto once in awhile. Otherwise, the ghetto will always remain the ghetto and, hence, the true meaning of freedom will not be achieved.

These shortcomings are the conditions in the United States, which is the most powerful nation on the earth. Imagine, then, the conditions in other nations. In many countries, women are treated as second-class citizens, people are only allowed to believe in one religion, freedom of speech or media is nonexistent, and discrimination of all sorts are the laws of the land. An old, barbaric ruling system is in charge, controlling people's behaviors on the left and on the right. The economic machine turns at a corner where the governments decide, and the money flows where they plan for it to flow. The citizens have very little say in those countries because there is no freedom of speech.

We have come a long way from Cyrus's kingdom, but conditions in many countries remain the same or worse.

# 30

# The Minimum Wage Increase

There seems to be a sympathetic feeling in the United States among some political officials for minimum wage earnings. This sympathetic feeling appears in their speeches, often offering a proposal to increase the minimum wage. It is difficult to know what the intentions of these politicians are. Do they wish to help the poor as they claim? Or do they hope to garner votes? Regardless of their intentions, a minimum wage increase always works against the minimum wage earners. Whereas, raising the minimum wage may seem like a quick fix, over the long run, doing so has usually been disadvantageous to the poor. Nevertheless, a minimum wage increase will always be advantageous to the government, and it will open the door to a higher rate of earning for the government. History clearly shows that, after a minimum wage increase, the government collects much more in taxes than it did before the increase, and relatively, the only beneficiary of the wage increase was the government.

A minimum wage increase is not a way to help the poor. Rather, it makes the conditions a lot worse, given that the concurrent price increases are always greater than that of the minimum wage. For example, let's go back to 1970. The minimum wage was about $1.65 per hour. At the same time, the price of an average house in Glendale California was about $27,000. To rent the same house, you would have to pay about $165 per month. The price of a gallon of gasoline was about $0.26, a pack of cigarettes was $0.35, and it cost $0.06 to mail an envelope.

In comparison, the minimum wage today is about $9 per hour. The price of the same house in Glendale is about $825,000. It costs around $3,000 a month to rent that house. A gallon of gasoline costs about $3, a pack of cigarettes is around $5.50, and you can mail an envelope for about $0.40.

Thus, we can clearly see that in 1970, it was possible for a minimum wage earner to buy a house. Today, for a minimum wage earner to buy a house is an impossibility, an overreaching dream. A minimum wage earner is not even able to rent a similar house.

To illustrate who is the real beneficiary in a wage increase occurrence, we can refer to the following example, assuming a 15 percent income tax is applicable.

| Year | Minimum Wage Rate | Payable Tax Rate | Taxes Paid |
|------|-------------------|------------------|------------|
| 1970 | $1.65 | 15% | $0.25 |
| 2013 | $8.00 | 15% | $1.20 |
| | | | =$0.95 |

The difference, in terms of the additional collected taxes from a minimum wage earner, is $0.95 per hour. Moreover, the above chart only shows the exceeding revenue collected per hour and maybe times million or billion hours worked in a given period. One can imagine the greater amount of taxes collected by the government. There is nothing wrong with the government collecting more taxes, as the government has many projects to fund. These projects are very significant. They function as a bloodstream for the economy and are especially important to those who receive a paycheck from the government every month. However, the discussion here is not about the government but, rather, about poor people, whose quality of life has been deteriorating over and over by minimum wage increases.

Despite all the sympathetic feelings of elected or unelected officials, considering inflation and other relative factors, is a minimum wage earner better off today or was he or she better off forty years ago?

# 31

# The $17 Billion Question

I occasionally hear the phrase if is, is is or if is, is not is and I always wonder what it means. If *is* really means *is*, then, how can it not be *is*? These days, the Bank of America's settlement with the Justice Department of $17 billion reminds me if is, is is or if is is not. Of course, this phrase was used as everybody remembers by our beloved former president Clinton during the Monica Lewinsky investigation. Nevertheless, it makes me wonder if this world we live in is real or if there is another world that I am not aware of or cannot see.

At the end of August 2014, Bank of America agreed to pay $17 billion for a crime it appears it did not even commit, and that is the question. During the financial crisis, Bank of America was one of the healthiest financial institutes in the United States. It had acquired two firms with lots of toxic assets in 2008 sometimes during the financial crisis. These institutions initiated a major role in the financial crisis, especially Countrywide. The CEO of a bank such as Bank of America is not a person within ordinary IQ. To be in the position of such a huge organization, a person must be extremely intelligent and able to make decisions that are beneficial to the bank's interests. Obviously, the same goes for the board members. Each is most likely a very intelligent individual. Even an ordinary person like me would have known better than to invest in Countrywide, which was full of toxic assets at the time. So, how is it that the intelligent people running Bank of America made such a mistake?

Merrill Lynch was another almost broke financial institute that Bank of America had to acquire—for a little over twenty-nine dollars per a share. Each share of Merrill Lynch was not worth twenty-nine dollars at the time, and this purchase was a shock to the financial world at the time. Bank of

America was a clean financial institution and did not need to be involved in purchasing Countrywide and Merrill Lynch. The world that we live in does not seems as black and white as we visualize it to be. Either the CEO and the board members of Bank of America were really greedy, or there are other facts that we are not aware of.

# 32

# Women And Man

It is troubling that, even in the United States, the most advanced civilization in the world, women are still victims of discrimination and earning less than men for doing the same job. At the same time, it's delightful to see that women are becoming successful in the United States, evidenced by the fact that many great companies have a female CEO at their head, among them IBM, PepsiCo, Yahoo, and GM. For the first time, the prospect of a female president is in the horizon, as Hillary Clinton is campaigning for the job today. Her election would be, of course, an event that would change history and a demonstration that, finally, progress is being made toward achieving meaningful equality. Even though she lost the election, her entering in the race is a historic event. Janet Yellen's name is also worth mentioning, as she is a most qualified chair of the Board of Governors of the Federal Reserve System.

Looking at other parts of the world, we can see that woman are treated as second-class citizen or used as merchandize. In some places, women aren't allowed to drive or take part in all sectors of society, and they often encounter existing discrimination laws that preventing them from receiving equal treatment. In some parts of the world, a woman must walk behind her husband or eat the leftovers after he finishes eating! As the West is advancing to recognize the rights of woman, other parts of the world must come to the reality that women have the right to equal treatment and to equal rights.

I read somewhere in internet that a nine year old girl died due to sexual bleeding caused by her forty year old husband somewhere in the world this year. It is a shame if this is a legitimate news and it is a shame that it did not become the biggest news in the media.

It is customary in the United States that a man open the passenger door for a woman and help her enter the car. It is customary for men to pick up the bill when dining out and pay for dating costs. It is also customary for a man to yield the right of way to a woman passing through a passage, entering a room, stepping into an elevator, and so forth. It has been wonderful to see these adapted customs and mutual politeness throughout the years. Nevertheless, as equality is taking place, we see these customs less frequently within the younger generation, which is further indication that equality is moving toward reality.

Any expectations or customs most likely show that there is a definitively different set of rules for men and women in a society, and as long as these conditions exist, real equality cannot be obtained. In order to have true equality, all special treatments existing on either side must be demolished. Only then will equality be possible. It seems like a difficult task, but in order to achieve gender equality, conditions must be changed around the world.

# Iran And What You May Not Know About It

# 33

# Persia Or Iran

It is interesting for many perhaps to know why the ancient name Persia changed to the modern name Iran. In order to provide a clear picture, it is necessary to review the beginning of history to see how it all began. The German philosopher Georg Wilhelm Friedrich said, "The Persians are the first historical people". The Medes unified Persia as a nation in 625 BC. Cyrus the Great (600 - 530 BC) overthrow the Medes, Lydian and Babylonian creating the largest Empire in history. He liberated the Jews from captivity and helped them to rebuild their temples in Jerusalem. He also wrote the Tablet of Freedom telling all humankind are free to worship any God or any religion that they want. Cyrus's son Cambyses conquered Egypt the last power and the Persians expanded their Empire to Africa. Darius the Great (522 - 486 BC) had an ambition to facilitate roads and shortened the sea traveling. He constructed a canal enabling two ships to pass through at the same time between the Nile River and the Red Sea, which led eventually to the Suez Canal in the modern world. The Persians created a world government lasting for two and a half centuries (650 - 330 BC) spanning three continents Asia, Europe and Africa.

According to the earliest archaeological artifacts found in Iran human life existed a 100,000 years ago. Archaeological artifacts found in Kerman, Kermanshah, Khorramabad, around Alborz and Zagros Mountains are indicating the ancient civilization where Iranian people resided during the early Iron Age early as 20,000 BC.

Alexander the Great put a pause in continuation of this super power empire. However, less than a century later Persian dynasties took over governing the plateau all over again. First dynasty was Parthian (247 BC - 224 CE) that stopped the aggression of Rome on the East Side. They were culturally influential and 100 years BC introduced Europe to Mithraism that was worshipped by the Romans and most parts of Europe for four centuries. During Constantine 300 CE, it became a forbidden religion and replaced by Christianity. The second dynasty was Sasanian (224 - 651 CE) that their territories expanded to Egypt time to time.

It is important to mention that Iran is a non-Arabic country, during Islam invasion (651 - 819 CE) and thereafter science in math, physics, medicine, astrology and chemistry flourished in Persia. However, history calls this duration "The Golden Age of Arab Civilization" when majorities of the scientists were all Persians! I do not see justice here and I think the Persians should have recognition and credit for the world science advancements. Persia also introduced the world with literature like never before. Works of Omar Khayyam, Firdausi, Rumi, Saadi, Hafez, Sanaie, Nizami, Rodaki and so many more are witnesses of this duration.

Saadi, whose words became a guideline for the United Nations and are written at its entrance. Rumi, whose message of love offers meaning to life. Hkayyam, whose Rubaiyats translated in more than 70 languages. Hafez, whose poets inspired the imagination of so many writers such as Victor Hugo, Andre Gide, Armando Renaud and others in the modern world.

Moving alone to why Persia was Iran. In 1935, there was a name change to correspond with the land where the Aryans lived. Iran as spelled in Farsi (Iranian language) contains this meaning but the way it is spelled in most languages, it does not carry on such a meaning, unfortunately and that is yet another historical mistake.

# 34

# Iran, Home Of Many Tribes

One day, I was thinking of the economic jungle of our world, and it occurred to me that, if outsiders take away everything else from us Iranians, in the end, abundant volumes of poems and literature as an ocean of poetry, as well as a rich history and a magnificent culture will remain, still belong to us. Iran is a culture that contains high achievements, especially in literature, which has reached its highest level possible. To prove the reality of such a claim, it is enough to point out some of the men responsible, such as Rudaki, Daqiqi, Anvari, Ansuri, Gorgani, Sanai, Nizami, Iraqi, Omar Khayyam, Ferdowsi, Manuchihri, Jami, Baba Tahire Oryon, Khaqani, Sistani, Samrqandi, Ibn-e-Sina, Kermani, Attar, Sadie, Rumi, Hafiz, Vahshi Bahghi, Saeb Tabrizi, Hatef, and hundreds of other poets and writers, each creating incomparable masterpieces that shine in the world of literature. Dante, Shakespeare, Tolstoy and many others have mentioned in their works that were influenced and/or inspired by one or few Persian poets such as Sadie, Hafiz, Rumi or others from this encompassing source of literary.

Alongside this ocean of poetry, the art of storytelling came into its existence, creating masterpieces such as 'Sinbad Nowmeh", "Bakhteyar Nowmeh", *Shahnameh,* "Jam-e-ul Hekayat", "Kalylo Damneh", *One Thousand and One Nights*, "Lila and Majnoon', "Farhad and Shirin" and hundreds of others, each remaining to shed light onto this giant city of literature and all proof for such a claim that Iran has produced litrary geniuses. This rich storytelling culture was mixed with various sciences, such as physics, math, medicine, chemistry, astrology, and philosophy to carry out the responsibility of advancing the civilization before and, specifically, after Islam. Promoting self-recognition in various matters of spirituality brought about Sufism, with different doctrines and schools of thought around spiritual achievements and unrepresented philosophical concepts after Islam.

A unique history of over two and half millenniums started shortly before the mighty Hakamanid, who ruled the world for two centuries, and soon after Alexander's attack was taken to the Parthians, the Sassanians, the Samanians after Islam, the Seljuks, and other dynasties ruling the Middle East and Central Asia until the appearance of the new civilizations four centuries ago. Though great turbulence was on its way, somehow Iran picked up the pieces and continued making vast contributions to today's advancements.

I was in this frame of mind when, with a great appetite or curiosity, I began searching for such a great civilization in English textbooks and history books, as well as in general information sources, almanacs, and the like. The more I looked, the less I found words containing the existence of such a giant literary civilization. In the end, I realized that, with the exception of limited peoples outside of Iran and we Iranians, no one knows nor is informed about the existence of such an impactful and influential civilization. I thought to myself that, perhaps in translations, this wealthy inheritance was looted, and this mass of contributions to civilization was attributed to other nationalities.

Within the realm of this civilization lived many different people, different races, different tribes, and different clans and social groups, each speaking different languages. Yet they lived in harmony and peace. The beauty of this nation is the diversity of its citizenry, which still exists, and it is a joy to go from one corner to another visiting different tribes, a member of each tribe different from others and from you, and yet he or she is your brother or sister in his heart. For thousands of years, this is how it was, and the same continues to be true now after thousands of years. Tribes that are different from each other, in reality, are close to each other and have lived next to each other for millenniums.

Nevertheless, during Iranian history, a family of a tribe rose up against a weak ruling dynasty and took over the kingdom, and that is how it was from the beginning of the time. The name of some tribes, clans, or social groups include Balouch, Bakhtiyar, Fars, Gilak, Lour, Kurd, Tajik, Turk, Turkestán, Uzbek, Afghan, and perhaps others. Consequently, it is important to point out that kingdom dynasties of Turkish clans, such as the Ghaznavids and Seljuks in Iran after Islam, is definitely part of Iran's history without any conceptions that have appeared in the English version of history. The perception is that, during the Ghaznavids and Seljuks, Persian poetry and literature had blossomed and reached its highest zeal. Many great Persian poets were living at this time, and the Persian language, little by little, was replacing other languages.

These two kingdoms were able to redeem most lost territories, and they created a power that lasted a few centuries. Given that these two dynasties were so crucial and so significant to Iran's history, it is difficult to understand English-language history, which considers this fruitful duration of Iran's history a period of domination by the Turks. Consider that neither did the dynasties promote the Turkish language nor did there exist any nation called Turkey to "dominate other nations." When we read words such as *domination* in Farsi in regard to the Turkish dynasties, it means something different than it does in English, which misleads the minds of readers. The Ghaznavids and Seljuks or other Turkish dynasties who were involved with Iranian history definitely belonged to Iran and cannot be separated from Iranian history as is demonstrated in the English language which seems as Iran was taken over by none Iranians.

This was a civilization whose realm was vast for thousands of years, until it encountered modern civilization and most of its vast territories, which had everlasting historical and cultural ties, were taken away from it. Approximately two hundred years ago, a new addition was made to the civilization when Russia, by tinkering and taking advantage of an incompetent dynasty, denounced the rulers and enticed them to sign shameful treaties, called Gulistan in 1813 and Turkemanchay in 1828, resulting in devastating loss for Iran. This area included Georgia, Azerbaijan, Armenia, the North Caucasian of Daghestan and the north of River Aras Iranian territory occupied by Russia in 19th century. Territories where the Persian language was the main literacy language of correspondence in Central Asia were occupied by Russia's forces and were lost to Russia, which could not even speak the language. At the time that the whole world was advancing, unfortunately, in Iran, deterioration was taking place. Filthy, nasty kings had twenty or thirty wives in their harems and did not have time to advance or defend the country, and that is a shame. One of these nasty kings was said to have two hundred children. This kingdom

(Qajar) was perhaps as bad as the attack of Genghis Khan, maybe even worse for Iran. The last part taken away from Iran by the forces of the new civilization was the island of Bahrain.

This civilization founded backgammon, an internationally played game. And yet, the game's roots are not recognized by anyone, and when crediting the game makers for its introduction, historians look from one side to the other side and remark that its origin is unknown or name many other countries but never Iran. No one knows the story of backgammon or about its founder, Bozorgmehr, the prime minister of Anoushiravan and king of Sassanians before Islam.

Not many people recognize that drinking wine, despite perceptions that wine is a product of France, Germany, Italy, Russia, Spain or some other Western countries, originated in Persia—though it is strange to accept this fact looking at Iran of today. The eagle, symbol of freedom in the United States, also came from Persian from the patches on the uniforms of military men.

Not much is said about Persia in English language history after Alexander until Islam—a long period of time when Persian kingdoms ruled a vast geographical area for nine centuries. According to history, Persians were the only power able to clash with the Romans and defeat them almost every time they were attacked. Almost nothing is said about the might of the kingdoms who built the first university and contributed to civilization during the Romans as well. Nine centuries is a long time. For all that time, we do not hear much about the Persians. Rather, English-language history seems to center its focus on the Romans and their involvement with Christianity and its history.

This is a civilization whose internationaly known folkloric tales, Mulla Nasrudin, have been translated into English several times. But in many versions, the character is introduced as an international character belonging to many countries near Iran, and some versions don't even mentioned Iran. This directly contradicts the long history of these humorous tales in Iranian culture, which stretches back thousands of years.

This is a civilization that taught poetry and science to even its attackers, as is shown in history over and over. It is, perhaps, for this specific reason that the Abbasid caliphs changed their capital from Damascus to Baghdad, where Arabic was not a native language at the time, and Baghdad was a part of the Persian Empire. By this move and protection from some Sunni Persian dynasties, the Abbasid became the center of Islamic power and the world. They closed an existing Persian university said to be the oldest and the first in the world and opened one under their own name. That is how a so-called the Islamic Golden Age came about.

This is a civilization that, during the past three centuries, when other civilizations were becoming advanced, went to a deep sleep because of weakness, corruption, superstition, prejudice, ignorance, and directorship of imposing governments. In the past three centuries, the new comer mainly the Westerners took away valuable land, sea, wealth, history, even the civilization that once was growing insde of Iran.

This is a civilization whose history translated into English from other languages, such as Greek, Arabic, Turkish, Hindu, and others, confusing even us Iranian when it comes to our own history, when it's referred to in the English version. The name *Cyrus* replaces *Kourosh*; *Xerxes* is used for *Khashayar*; *Avicenna* is used instead of *Ibn-e-Sina*; and on and on. The defeat of Khashayar is talked about over and over, even brought the word marathon in humanity when he was defeated and a man ran to Greece to bering the news. There is not much said about his genius idea to construct a bridge over the Nile for the first time in history in the fourth century BC. His defeat of Greece is less significant and seldom talked about, but Alexander's victories are the center focus in every history book. This freedom that is given to the citizens of a nation seems to be a product of the modern world, but that is not so, as freedom was practiced and established during the fifth century BC by Koroush.

This civilization, which contributed so much to the advancements of the world, mostly to the Europeans, in return received nothing but looting and destruction. Adding insult to injury, knowledge and information about this civilization offered to Westerners is so limited that the average person has no idea about the existence of such a civilization. It is sad that the people in the West do not even know that the Mongols attacked Iran. It appears that they attacked Russia. I witnessed a television game host said the same exact words. Of course, it is not his fault. He was not educated to know better—to have the facts.

According to many historians, before the reign of Peter the Great (1698–1725), the conditions in Russia was largely medieval. Moreover, a while ago, I read a book called *Russia and the Russians* by Geoffrey Hosking. The book contains just over six hundred pages, and about fifty-two pages are designated to materials relating to the Mongols and the Russians. I did not find so much as a page or a paragraph explaining the reason for Genghis's aggregation and attack. I found no mention of the massacre in which three million people lost their lives, children and women were raped, and the Persians suffered other unthinkable horrors. I only found two brief lines mentioning the Khwarezmian Empire and Persia. According to this book, it seems like the Mongols' aim was Russia, which is not true. Genghis wanted to have a trading treaty with Ala ad Din Muhammad II, a king of Persia. When he did not received the agreement and his passengers were killed by the Persian king, he attacked, and horrible tragedy befell the Persian people and, later, others (a subject which we will refer to in pages ahead). *Russia and the Russians* refers many times to the Caspian Sea, but I am not certain if it reveals how that sea was snatched from Iran. The subject of central Asia is also discussed frequently, as well as a brief mention of Azerbaijan and west coast areas of the Caspian Sea—the same areas that once were all part of Persia.

Another point worth mentioning centers on nomenclature. It is as appalling to me now as it was in my youth, when I was living in Iran, that some of my family members or friends bore the names (or related names) of the destroyers of Iran (Persia), such as Escandar (Alexander), Changiz (Genghis), and others who killed vast numbers of Iranian citizens and attempted to destroy their culture. It is difficult to understand. For example, we do not see any Jewish males named Adolph Hitler now, after the Holocaust, which was the most shameful act against the Jew and humanity. Most likely, within the entire worldwide Jewish population, we would not find even one example of the name Adolph Hitler. In the case of the Iranians, all kinds of invaders' names are given to children; it is hard to digest. Furthermore, I do not recall hearing of any other nation customarily giving their children the names of their enemies!

However, no Iranian person with such a name is at fault. A name is given at childhood, and it is passed on from one generation to the next. I do not intend the pointing out of such a mystery as a character assassination of anyone with such names.

I do intent to point out that, all too often, when information is translated into English from other languages, that which is false is often made true, and truth become false, without much reliance on fact. We have allowed and we continue to allow the nonfactual to become factual and the factual to be buried under a pile of dust in history books.

Today, nobody who speaks English is aware of the mentioned facts above or if there is, it would be very limited people. However, people would become aware if they were informed. And if they are not, it is the fault of those who knew and did nothing about it.

Translated excerpts from literary and history books of Iran.

# 35

# Iran And Islam

The beliefs and religion of the Arabs before the founding of Islam are widely unknown. According to the Koran, there were many prophets before Muhammad teaching the oneness of God and the biblical approach to the creation by the Almighty God. In accordance with Islamic scripts and some remaining holy writings within Islam, the Arabs before Muhammad were either idol worshipers or practitioners of Judaism or Christianity. Many stories told of the Arabs burying their daughters alive at birth because they thought having a daughter was a shame. The picture is clear, before the Messenger of God, Muhammad, there was not much civilization within the Arab world. Speaking Arabic was limited to Saudi Arabia of today and perhaps a few islands around it. The founding of Islam changed all of these conditions, especially after the victorious war against the Persians. When Islam took over centuries of domination by the Persians, it took over half of the world thereof. Historically, the realm of the Persians extended from India to the Roman territories, and they were the only nation to defeat the Romans almost every time they were attacked.

When we review history, we find that, before Persia was invaded by the Arabs, the Persians had their own culture, tradition, and religion, worshiping a faith brought to them by Zoroaster, who lived several centuries before Christ. Though the Zoroastrian religion was worshiped in the world for centuries before Islam and centuries before Alexander, the conquest by Alexander, despite the fact it was aimed to do so, did not demolish the Zoroastrian religion, as was done by Islam. According to historians, Alexander had no respect for the Persian culture or its religion. He maliciously set fire to books mentioning Zoroaster's name or teachings. He also burned the greatest library of the time, as he had been taught by his childhood tutor Aristotle to do so when he was going to become victorious.

It is unknown how much knowledge the burned books—millenniums of data prior to Alexander—could offer us today. However, this is a separate subject altogether.

As a matter of fact and as the fact still remains today, Islam replaced all religions, including Zoroastrianism, in Iran. Even though there are still some followers of Zoroaster living in Iran, after the invasion of Islam, many left, looking for an alternative place to live. Today one can find their living generations in India, mostly around the city of Bombay (Mumbai).

As history is a witness, victorious Arabs robbed centuries of wealth belonging to the Persians. They also robbed wisdom and civilization by incapacitating, obstructing, defecting, demonizing, and diminishing the values of the Persian beliefs and traditions. There was not any human dignity and respect, given that the Arabs claimed to be representing a message from the God Almighty? If the message of God is love, execution of acts so shameful to mention is not love. I cannot accept that these actions were in any form or shape the message of Mohammed the Prophet of God or the message of God because God is nothing but love.

However, the Arab invasion thereafter caused the Arabic language to be learned in Iran, especially by the Persians scholars, as well as other people in the Middle East and northern African nations. Thereafter, a new chapter opened, and Islam became a turning point in history by the will of God as is believed to be.

Little by little, Islam had significantly changed the way of life and beliefs in Iran. Many philosophers, mathematicians, physicians, scientists, and writers believed that Islam was a religion delivered to them by God. To show their solidarity and faithfulness in Islam, they wrote their books and findings in Arabic. Other nationalist Muslim Iranian poets or writers tried to preserve the Persian language by avoiding the use of any Arabic words in their writings or poems. Such a poet is the famous storyteller Ferdowsi (940–1020), whose tireless ambitions are printed in his remaining book, *Shahnameh*. He dedicated nearly thirty years of his life to composing the *Shahnameh*, an epic of about 60,000 couples perpetuating the history of dynasties and kingdoms before Islam. It is said that Persian-speaking people around the world owe their language to Ferdowsi, a man who, despite all odds and suffering, never gave up until his work was done. This tireless effort to revive the Persian language was recognized years ago by

UNICEF, when the program recognized *Shahnameh* as the world's greatest story collection preserving the Persian language.

During the Arab invasion, which last for centuries, scientific discoveries in geography, logic, philosophy, algebra, mathematics, astronomy, chemistry, and medicine by Persian scholars became mixed with those Arab scholars—due to the fact that Persian scholars also chose to write their books and findings in Arabic. This choice causes a mass of confusion to this day. Though nothing is wrong with selecting to publish in a language different than your own, just as is done today with the English language around the world, it would be wrong to henceforth call all the people writing in English American or English. This is what happened in Persia. By selecting Arabic as the language of publication, Persian scholars unwittingly changed how they would be remembered by history, and all of their writings eventually "belonged" to the Arabs or Islam.

This confusion came into history at a crucial time—a time referred to as the Arabic or Islamic Golden Age—and was then carried on until today. For example, textbooks in the United States today contain chapters that give much mention and recognition to Arabic or Islamic contributions. Though there is no possible way that I can deny that there were not brilliant wise scientists with Arabic origin during the Arabic blossom, however, many of these contributions were made by Persian scholars as well. This does not give a clear picture in history books today and never did. Because hundreds of books written by Persians in Arabic language were credited to Arabs or to Islam. If we are living in a society in which fairness is important, then the credit must go where the credit is due. A study can be done to reveal a vision with a correct percentages of the Persian contributors to this regard to clarfy this significant historic confusion.

Following is a short list of the names of some of those scientist and scholars who contributed immensely to the new civilization during the so-called Islamic Golden Ages:

- *Khwarizmi* (780–850) was a mathematical genius and the founder of algebra. He worked on astronomy, geography, astrology, and under him in 830 the 1st globe map was produced.
- *Ibn-e-sina* (980–1037) (Latinized as *Avicenna*), the father of modern medicine, wrote 450 books, 40 of them on medicine.

*The Canon of Medicine* and *The Book of Healing* are the two of his most famous books. His books on medicine are taught in European universities.

- *Omar Khayyam* (1048–1131) was a master of mathematics and poetry.

Among the scholars, it is important to include the magical tales of *One Thousand and One Nights*, a collection of tales including "Aladdin's Wonderful Lamp," "Ali Baba and the Forty Thieves," and "The Seven Voyages of Sinbad the Sailor," told by Scheherazade, the king's wife, to the king, Shahryar, in exchange for her life. His compelling and imaginative tales would contribute greatly to the future of storytelling and remain an inspiration over a thousand years after they were written. Sadly enough, this collection has historically been and still continues to be introduced as an Arabic writing, with a tempering Arabic name *The Arabian Nights*, when the main character's name is Shahryar, a Persian name. Most likely, changes to make it appear as an Arabian tale occurred during Harun al Rashid, the Abbasid caliph, when the collection of stories was translated to Arabic. Nevertheless, it is believed that the source of the *Nights* is the Hazar Afsana (a Thousand Tales) coming from the Sassanid Empire before Islam. Perhaps it would be most suitable if its name were to change to *The Persian Nights*. The tales are also a rich source of storytelling in Hollywood, especially for the cartoon industry.

Some other brilliant men, among them the founder of the use of alcohol for medicinal purposes, can be remembered as truly great scholars. These include Farabi (870–950), Zakariya Razi (854–925), Zahiri, Ghazali, Berovni, Jami, Anvari, Sanai, Attar, Sadi, Hafiz, Rumi, and many other outstanding thinkers who kept the light on during a medieval era when all other civilizations were asleep in the so-called Dark Ages. Their knowledge, stories, talent and wisdom were passed on to the modern world, where their identities and contributions were often assigned to other nations or identities, rather than Iran (Persia).

Despite new technologies and advancements, this unfair treatment continues reboiled the old information into the new data sources. If one searches online for *Khwarizmi*, the results will suggest that Khwarizmi is an Islamic figure.

It is a shame that history is lost in millenniums where light became dark and dark became light. This is what happened when it comes to the history of the Persians, their culture, their civilization, and their immeasurable influences on modern civilization, all of which was either robbed, rendered unknown, or lost in translation.

Somebody may ask me, why am I writing about contributions made by Iran? And, why is not my focus for example on America? My answer would be that America does not need my writings about its achievements. Everybody knows about them and everything is documented well. In regard to Iran, there are not much information available and it is the exact opposite of America. My intend is not to compare Iran with America and one can see that perhaps 90 percent of all advances occurred within the last hundred years. America can be credited for a great percent of these advancements. However, it is also significant to know about the past and the role of Iran in it.

Extracted and translated from literary and Iranian history.

# 36

# Resurrection

If there is such a thing as resurrection or life after death, I am the example of it. I lived two thousand five hundred years ago with the ideas of the prophet Zoroaster, who with his Ahuramazda and a beautiful angel named Anahita has dominated the minds of men and women.

Anahita was depicted as a beautiful and strong woman, with prominent breasts, a golden crown of stars, and golden raiment. She is worshipped as the goddess of generations. At her side stands the sun god Mithras, who is presented as a young and victorious hero. I am at the site of Cyrus's architectural works in Pasargad. The Aryan nation started its history here.

I am Persian goddess Later, by traveling to Greece and receiving some minor name changes, I became the well-known Greek goddesses of mythology.

Here at Pasargad, Zoroaster is worshipped. He has three religious principles—good thoughts, good deeds, and good words. If we were able to follow these three simple teachings, perhaps we would not need to go to a priest to confess, as there would be no sin to be confessed.

I also lived almost nine hundred years ago, inside a different story of characters created by different writers. I am Aladdin, a character in a story of Alef-Layla-wa-Layla. I am also Ali Baba, a thief who robs from the rich in order to feed the poor. I am a sailor named Sinbad in a book called Sinbad-nama. I am a collection of history.

I was also in the presence of Rumi, when Rumi wrote the following poem:

*I died as mineral and become a plant,*
*I died as plant and rose to animal,*
*I died as animal and I was human,*
*Why should I fear? When was I less by dying?*

*Yet once more I shall die human,*
*To soar with angels blessed above.*
*And when I sacrifice my angel soul*
*I should become what no mind ever conceived.*
*As a human, I will die once more,*
*Reborn, I will with the angel soar.*
*And when I let my angel body go,*
*I shall be more than moral mind can know.*

I am in the body of a dervish Sufi who is following the Sufis' paths, saying Moses experienced what the Sufis call *fana*, complete annihilation in the truth of self certainty, followed by *baqa*, the eternal subsistence in God. His sandals represented his separation from the creator. When Moses reached the burning bush, he was called by name, "O Moses! Verily I am the Lord. Take off the sandals. Verily thou art in the holy valley of Tuma."

Why is humanity interested in the magic flying carpet? Where do they think it will carry them? To a land of fantasy or to a place outside of themselves, where each being has inner peace and freedom?

Humanity is the magic flying carpet, and the ability to fly, to rise above all things, completes the weaving process of the carpet.

If there is a resurrection, I am the example of it. I am sitting next to the master Mahatma Gandhi and learning the words of wisdom.

I am also walking side by side with Galileo. He tries to prove to the church that the earth is not flat but it is round. They do not believe him.

I was also here with the Wright brothers who finally brought to reality the idea of magic flying carpet and flew for the first time.

If there is a resurrection, I am the survivor of it, as repeats in history over and over. I am nobody but mankind.

Sources: Encyclopedia Britannica, and Discovering Cyrus.

# 37

# The Persian Genocides

Whether or not *genocide* is the correct word to describe the Persians difficulties in history is my question. If genocide can refer to the destruction of a cultural, political, or racial group, then it is definitely the correct word to describe the plight faced, over and over throughout history, by the Persians. On the other hand, perhaps wars between nations, though they bring destruction, cannot be considered genocide. However, by looking at history, we can see that no nation has suffered as much as that of the Persians.

To mention some of these tragedies and sufferings, we find monumental advancements in art, science, and literature and a centralized civilization destroyed and a vast massacre committed by Temujin, "Genghis Khan" of Mongolia. The trigger for this massacre was a business accord proposed by Genghis Khan to Shah Ala ad-Din Muhammad of the Khwarazmian dynasty, which was vigorously or violently rejected. Genghis attacked Persia, accompanied by his sons and two hundred thousand soldiers. The Shah miscalculated the size of the army of Temujin and divided his army into smaller groups to protect various cities. This decision reduced security, and in 1220, Temujin became victorious over the Persian king. He ordered people of cities such as Samarkand to evacuate the city, then he killed them and made pyramids of their heads. He killed more than 1.3 million people, which is considered one of the bloodiest massacres in human history. The young women and children were given to the Mongolian soldiers as slaves, while the rest of population was massacred. No certain or actual number of people killed by Genghis in Persia was recorded. Therefore, the estimations vary from 1.2 to 3 or 4 million. After Genghis's death, his heirs stayed and imposed themselves as rulers over Persia (Iran). They learned the language, practiced Islam and thereafter become part of the Persian history.

This draws raise a question in my mind. *Why* does not the data and average knowledge in America or Europe reveal that Genghis became a so-called great conqueror after his victory over the Persians? Because the existing information is not clear and misleading. It seems that Western accounts of Genghis center on Russia, which at the time was not even form as a great nation. other Eastern European countries, which one way or other came into the focus of the Mongolians, did not have much of central government neither. Therefore, in my opinion, because the Western version of history was mainly translated from other languages into English did not form a clear picture and this is an example which can reveal such a misleading of information. Nevertheless, to obtain accurate information we can refer to, "Jami al-tawarikh", which is called, "The First World History". It was written by R. Hamadani (1247-1318). It is unknown to me if an English translation of this history book is available.

Moving forward to a further examination of historical events, we encounter the the Arabs invasion of Persia and the destruction of the world's greatest civilization of the time. The Arabs attacked Persia three times. When finally, on the third attempt, during Omar the second caliph, they were victorious, they looted jewelry gifted to the Persian kings accumulated in centuries. Thereafter, this massive source of wealth became the source of finance to advance Islam. To obliterate the teachings of Zoroaster was to obliterate Persian religion and culture, as well as its influences. If definition of genocide is cultural, racial, and political destruction this is a clear example of it.

To continue this constant destruction we can see the Abbasid caliphates moved their capital from Damascus to Baghdad, where Arabic language was not spoken at the time. A caliph named Harun al-Rashid closed the world's very first university of its kind, "Jondi Shapour," and constructed a replacement in Baghdad. This university was built by King Shapour of the Sassanids in the fourth to fifth centuries AD until it was abandoned by the Abbasids.

After Persia (Iran) became an Islamic nation, either by the Will of God or the course of history, it contributed immensely to the success of Islam. This success was either by territorial advancement or progression in sciences—math, physics, chemistry, astronomy, and medicine—as well as in philosophy, art, and literature, primarily of Persian scholars whose writings were in Arabic language.

It is important to mention that, when the dust settled and the Muslims entered the Crusades Wars with the Europeans, the Muslim kings involved in the Crusades were all historically heirs of the Iranian dynasties. This fact, however, for some unknown reason, is also hidden in English language and history books, as well as other texts in America. This dynasty (the Seljuk) were of Turkish descent, and their grandparents migrated to Iran, serving in palaces as slaves. After a generation or two, they became Iranian citizen. When the opportunity arrived, they took over the kingdom and carried out a major part of the Iranian history after Islam.

Alexander is one of the most fomous conquerors in history. Perhaps, one of the significant turning points that changed the direction of history was the victory of Alexander over the Achaemenids, who ruled the world for centuries, established the method of governing for the first time in history, circulating minted coins and pioneered the civilization. Alexander, from childhood, was a student of Aristotle, who disliked Persian domination. Thus, Alexander was taught that, in order to be a great leader, he had to fight and defeat the Persians. It is said that Alexander's army was much smaller than and could not face that of the Persians, but in order to win, he bought important secrets from a perpetrator whom he killed after his victory. When Alexander became victorious, he burned the largest library of the time and destroyed any signs of civilization that he found in Persia, which was a dream come true. Alexander destroyed a civilization and the very first monotheistic religion found in the world (Zoroastrianism). This was, in a real sense, devastating and Alexander's victory brought great suffering to the Persians. There is a statement that says plate was the greatest philosopher but he with his teach learned it from the Persians. There is also a statment that Pythagoras had studied math under Zoroastrians. Author K.E. Eduljee in his book Zoroastrian Heritage mentions "Alexander jealous of unparalled knowledge of Persian nation, first translated what he needed from the Persians, then destroyed the rest…". Who knows what the world would look like today if Alexander had been defeated in Persia? Alexander was an openly gay man, who had a male lover but married a young princess in Persia. This unsettling condition of dealing with his gay lover and his wife created predicaments, and due to this or other conflicts, he was poisoned and killed while still in his youth in Persia. The territory he'd captured was divided among his generals to rule and govern after his death.

Despite all these tribulations throughout history, Iran survived. However, due to the ignorance of a recent century's ruling dynasty (Qajar), many states located in the north of Iran were given away to Russia in exchange for jewelry, gemstones, and sometimes young ladies gifted to the kings. Iran lost states where, for millenniums, people spoke Persian and that, for generations before, were part of its realms. States that are burial places of many wise men, scholars, and great poets of Iran, such as Omar Khayyam.

Later, under the Communist Party, isolation came into effect, to a point that traveling to or from the nation, as well as even speaking Persian, was not allowed. Right about this time, a great half of the Caspian Sea was given away to Russia by a king who said, "We do not need that salty water." I do not know how much stupidity is enough. Changes made in modern history, as well as the existence of a weak central government, have been more or equally as devastating to Iran.

If there have been such thing as a Persian genocide, history, during its course, has seen it repeated over and over. The most influential of these— the genocide by the Arabs that indeed cleansed forever the racial, cultural, and political manner of a group—is visible even today.

One hopes that the current round of violence will stop and that religion, which aims at love, unity, and brotherhood, will be used only for these divine purposes, rather than for division, separation, war, and invasion.

Translated excerpts from Iran's History Books.

# 38

# The Story Of Divorce

There is a religious law in Islam called Mohalel, which basically means that you divorce your wife by saying three times, "I divorce you" (an optional way to obtain a divorce). However, if you change your mind, you cannot marry your divorced wife again unless another man marries and divorces her.

There was a clergyman who had an office in a town called Qulhak that was one of the major bus stops north of Tehran, where I used to go to high school. Under the clergyman's second-story office, there was a grocery and a toy store, as well as many other businesses. There was a rumor that the grocery owner was having problems with his wife. The clergyman constantly told the merchant that he should divorce her, and at last, the merchant agreed.

The pure and innocent wife received her divorce. The grocer optioned for the kind of divorce that required him to thrice repeat the phrase "I divorce thee," and it was performed by the local clergyman.

As the time passed, the merchant realized his mistake and went back to his ex-wife, asking her for forgiveness. After a long time, which included much back and forth and, ultimately, a great deal of begging, she finally agreed to remarry the merchant. However, there was a problem. Because she had been divorced under the law of Mohalel, the couple was prohibited from remarrying. They turned to the clergyman for advice and a solution. They thought he was the most trusted and worthy person around who could help them.

They offered to donate some money for a good religious cause, so the clergyman would help them, by fulfilling the Mohalel's requirement of another marriage and then divorcing the wife so she and the merchant could remarry. The clergyman, who'd probably planned all of this all along, married her and never divorced her. No matter what the woman did or what the merchant did, he refused to divorce her.

It was said that the lady was a beautiful woman, and perhaps it was the best way for a fat, ugly, and short man to acquire a beautiful wife.

I have seen places where children have very little to eat, but one can see kindness and the biggest smiles all over their faces. I have also seen places where children eat as much as they want, and there is little kindness or smiles on the people's unkind faces, as if the whole world owes them something. Strangely enough, I have never seen in any other place anything like the story of the Mohalel.

## 39

# The United States And Iran In The Past And The Future

Tension between the United States and Iran has lasted for over three decades. This conflict started after the Shah's regime ended in 1978. The demolishing of a configuration of dynastic rule in Iran was a historical event and one of great importance to world history. The kingdom dynasty form of ruling, which still exists in different forms in different parts of the world, was established around 2,500 years ago by mighty kings, such as Cyrus the Great, Darius, Xerxes, and other Achaemenid kings as a way of ruling in Iran and, henceforward, in the many other nations. Though there were kings before the Achaemenid dynasty, ruling and governing a large geographical area began with the Achaemenids. This kingdom system of governing Iran, which off and on governed most parts of the Middle East for over 2,500 years, eventually ended by the overthrow of the latest Shah Mohammad Reza Pahlavi, and the dynasty ruling regime in Iran went into the pages of history.

The Shah was said to be the "island of stability" in the Middle East, but behind the curtain, the plans were to remove him from power, and he was indeed removed.

As an outsider and one who has no interest in political involvement, I am only expressing my observations, which may or may not bear the truth. However, the integral idea behind expressing these observations and learned knowledge is primarily a hope for improvement in diplomatic relation between Iran and the United States, soon before any perilous conditions, where it is usually average people, and not members of governments, who are going to suffer.

It is doubtful that there would be a war between the United States and Iran. It would not be beneficial to either side. Nevertheless, it is not my desire to see another war where many innocent people will be killed. I would not like to see the land where I grew up destroyed as has happened in Iraq. I was and still am against the war in Iraq, and to me, the end never justified this war. How many American soldiers lost their lives? How many innocent Iraqi civilians lost their lives? How many houses, streets, businesses, historical buildings, and priceless artifacts were either looted or destroyed in Iraq? How much money is this war going to cost the Iraqi citizens? How much will it cost the American taxpayers to care for thousands of young American soldiers crippled in Iraq and to rebuild Iraq? How about the financial support for the families of the beloved soldiers who lost their sweet, young lives in this meaningless war? What about their children who will never see their fathers or their mothers again? And for what?

To begin writing about conflict between the United States and Iran— seemingly an everlasting dilemma, or about fifty years (how many years does one live?)—I would like to thank our beloved former President Bill Clinton for his statement regarding Iran. Mr. Clinton explained very frankly what had happened to the people of Iran in the past fifty years due to certain foreign policies of the United States. President Clinton explained what happened when Iran had a chance to have a democracy in 1953. The popular leader, Dr. Mossadegh, was overthrown by the United States, and the Shah, who had fled Iran, was brought back and restored to power in order to protect US interests there.

In order to give a brief history of the US–Iranian relationship, we need to go back to the War World II and recall that the Allied Forces marched through Iran to face the Germans in Russia. The Germans were eventually defeated. Reza Shah Pahlavi, a hero of modern Iran, who had sided with Hitler, was captured and sent into exile, where he died. His son, Mohammad Reza Pahlavi, was placed in power as the new Shah by the coalition forces. It is said in Iran that Iran was the bridge to victory in War World II, but I am not sure about such a title, for I never have encountered such a title given to Iran by the English language or outside of Iran.

Many statements have been made about the Shah in both the United States and Iran. Due to the Shah's friendship with the United States, Iran was considered a Cold War ally, the Shah was portrayed as a nice guy, and he was protected for more than three decades.

Finally, it came the time that he had to be removed, and he was in 1978 during US President Jimmy Carter's administration. Of course, the United States denies any involvement and blames Ayatollah Khomeini for the downfall of the Shah. In reality, Ayatollah Khomeini was an exiled and forgotten old man until policies and benefits of some powerful foreign countries, led by the United States, united to remove the Shah. It was decided that the best person to replace the Shah and deflect the aggression of the Communist Party of the time in Russia was an Islamic leader. Who was loved by millions in Iran? Who was a better candidate than Ayatollah Khomeini? Audiotapes of Khomeini's speeches protesting the Shah's government began appearing all over Iran. Though he had protested for decades, before the implementation of this policy, his tapes were nowhere to be found. The Shah was forced to leave, and Khomeini was welcomed and gradually put in power, with a new system of Islamic government. Of course, the United States' plan backfired, as we all know the rest of the story.

If the Shah had been fair or had a regime based on justice for all, Ayatollah Khomeini had no chance. People were scared to converse with each other for fear that the person next to them might be a security service agent. The country was far from democratic during the Shah's regime. The wealth of the country was in the pockets of a few friends and relatives of the Shah, while many people lived in poverty. Outside the major cities, the great majority of people lived without electricity and even heating gas, while the abundant and valuable natural gas of the country was either wasted by being burned off or piped abroad. Many people did not even have clean drinking water and lived in primitive conditions.

The country's only sources of income were petroleum and agricultural products, limited to dried fruits and nuts or Persian rugs. Designs of Persian carpets were not protected. Nor were they copyrighted by the government or anyone. And these unique designs were made by machines outside of Iran for much cheaper prices. Iranian rug designs were given away to anyone to benefit from, without benefiting Iran. Basically, the country's economy depended on natural gas and crude oil. There was no other source of income created or planned for, and often, money was invested abroad instead of inside Iran.

Once in Iran, I saw a list of foreign companies that the Shah either had bailed out of bankruptcy or invested billions in, including Chase Manhattan, Dodge and Chrysler, Mercedes Benz, Pan-American Airways, and others. I cannot confirm the legitimacy of the list. Nevertheless, photocopies of it were circulating all over Iran at the time.

I also saw a list of people who took out money from Iran during or just before the Shah's departure some time in 1978. The list included many people close to the Shah, who each had wired millions of dollars out of the country. A hundred million dollars is a lot of money even today. One can imagine its power in 1978. Much of the wired money was invested in the United States, and it is said that one of the former Iranian government officials bought an amusement park located just north of Los Angeles years ago.

That is how it was for more than thirty years, and so much for the man who the United States had protected for decades, the man who overpowered Iran's angel of freedom, Dr. Mossadegh. The Shah monopolized the wealth of a rich country, dividing it among a limited few chosen people and leaving the majority of the population poor. He was a dictator who was in his own private world and out of touch.

It is said that, before his life was cut short, President Kennedy had a plan to remove the Shah. It is also said that President Nixon and the Shah were very close friends, and the Shah invested heavily in the election of Nixon over Kennedy and later McGovern. The Shah was also a close friend of David Rockefeller. It was said that the Shah lent a substantial amount of money to Rockefeller that could not be paid back and invested in his bank.

One of the major problems that stands in the way of normalization of relations between Iran and the United States is the resolution of the Iranian frozen assets.

However, the major problem between the two countries for almost two decades has been the growing pressure from the United States to force Iran to abandon its nuclear program. This predicament finally came to an end when, in 2015, the Obama administration stopped Iran from developing nuclear weapons. The same conflict existed between the Bush administration and Iran, and the same conflict existed between the Clinton administration and Iran, which extends to about two decades.

A question comes to mind. How long does it take to produce an atomic bomb? For some peculiar reason this is just taking too long compared to other nations, which had developed in the past. Secondly, gas and oil are the safest and maybe the least expensive source of energy, and Iran has almost unlimited resources. Why the need to scarify so much to gain so little? In the meanwhile, the United States has been selling weapons to Iran's neighboring countries at a highest speed. Are these events related to each other? Who knows? One may never know what goes on behind the curtain and between politicians. Discoveries may or may not come years later.

There is a lot said about our former President Bush, such as an almost full page of commentary printed in the opinion section of the *Los Angeles Times*, Sunday, January 11, 2004. Kevin Phillips seems to know precisely the history of the Bush family, from the time George H. W. Bush ran for the US Senate in 1964 from Texas to his being appointed the director of the CIA, all the way to his becoming the president of the United States and his ties with Middle Eastern royal families, as well as his links to the bin Ladens. Mr. Phillips described how Bush and his sons got involved with oil money and oil drilling in the Middle East and the Persian Gulf states. In reference to the Iran–Iraq War, Mr. Phillips writes, "The U.S. is known to have provided both biological cultures that could have been used for weapons and nuclear know-how to the regime." Furthermore, the article says, "Bush, operating largely behind the scenes through the 1980s initiated and supported much of the financing, intelligence and military help that built Saddam's Iraq into an aggressive power."

So much in the name of freedom and democracy!

Some of American–Iranian relation can be summarized as follows:

a) After War World II, Riza Shah Pahlavi, who had sided with Hitler, was captured and sent to exile by the coalition forces. His son was placed in power.

b) In 1953, a coup d'état was backed by the United States, bringing the Shah back.

c) The nationalist Dr. Mossadegh was captured and imprisoned, where he died.

d) For thirty years, the Shah invested Iranian money in various American companies.

e) Subsequently, the United States froze Iranian assets, including $11 billion in the United States.

f) In 1979, a popular revolt displaced the Shah after thirty years.

g) The 444-day hostage-taking by the students in Iran served no benefits to Iran.

h) The United States established and enforced international economic pressure and stopped trading with Iran.

i) i) The United States provided Saddam with biological and chemical weapons, which were used to kill an estimated 2 million Iranians in the Iran–Iraq War.

j) In 2007, a new sanction sought by the United States was passed by the UN to pressure Iran to stop its nuclear program. Officials in Iran stated that their uranium enrichment was for peaceful purposes. As long as other nations have nuclear facilities, they claimed, they could have the same rights.

k) A new sanction sought by Obama to minimize global trading with Iran forced many countries to search for other providers of crude oil and petroleum, rather than Iran. Though it became Obama's policy in 2013 to relax sanctions against Iran, the economy of Iran had already detrimentally suffered due to these sanctions.

l) Obama's administration, with its European counterparts, came to an agreement with Iran over its nuclear program in 2015 and released the frozen Iranian assets. Based on this agreement, Iran agreed to stop uranium enrichment and to ship all its enriched uranium outside of Iran.

These were the major issues between Iran and the United States that ought to be resolved.

An article printed in the March 20, 2005, edition of the *Los Angeles Times*, concerned the Iranian population living in the United States and some of their professions—law, medicine, and so on. It told of some Iranians who were involved with the FBI or the CIA to spy for the United States against their native homeland. The article went on to say that the US government provided lots of money to these people to provide information. The article also said that a person walks with four cell phones trying to get information for the CIA or the FBI.

As history has shown, Alexander did not defeat the Persians; the perpetrators around the king defeated the Persians by selling crucial secrets to Alexander. Without them, a defeat would not have been possible, as the Persian forces were far superior to those of Alexander. It is not my intention to compare the United States of today to Alexander and his forces, and it would be foolish to compare the Iran of today to the Persia of then. I am only reminding those who would betray their country by sale of information that such betrayal of one's nation pride always remains a shameful act. The character of citizens and the system of government controls the destiny of nations. As in regard to Iran's destiny of recent decades, if it is not Russia, it is the United States, and if is not the United States, it is Russia's interferences keeping Iran among third world countries. Russia, also through contracts, is taking decades of natural gas for a steel-melt factory and billions of dollars for a nuclear reactor program, whose production is constantly postponed, costing Iran more and more money. Iran has been a wealthy country but one way or another much of this wealth has been wasted in the past sixty years. And that is how it goes!

As I mentioned at the beginning of this essay, I have no desire to be involved with politics, but I have a lot of feelings for my native land. That is the only motivation for my writings.

In conclusion, I hope for a normal relation between Iran and the United States. I hope for a political reestablishment that is advantageous to both countries, with mutual understanding, trust, and benefits to both sides, so Iran too can become an industrial country.

At the end it is essential to mention that, we talked about issues, subjects, advancements, predicaments, histories, policies, economic and social difficulties, and the achievements. Along the way, we told stories as well. Now we are approaching the end and still did not address in a direct form the question I asked at the beginning, "Who Is Right and Who Is Wrong in our World's Arena?". Even though this question is answered to over and over indirectly, however, if someone needs a direct answer, "the Equality of Humankid", as well as "the Equality of Man and Woman" of the Bahai Faith can be a good start.

www.ingramcontent.com/pod-product-compliance
Lightning Source LLC
Chambersburg PA
CBHW071157120626
46546CB00006B/2307